The Not-So-Nimble Needlework Book

by Iris Rosenthal

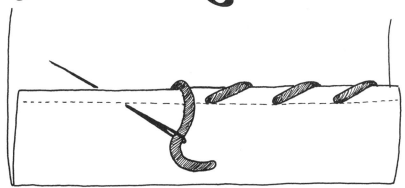

GROSSET & DUNLAP
A FILMWAYS COMPANY
Publishers • New York
Today Press

To my husband, Jules, for always encouraging my efforts and tolerating the clutter in our home during the preparation of this book.

First printing
Printed in the United States of America

Acknowledgments

I wish to express my gratitude to my dear friends and coworkers without whose help this book would not have materialized. Annabel Koota, whose dedication was steadfast during difficult times, and Mary Rutt, a talented young woman, whose ability as an artist in addition to her skill as a physical therapist helped solve many problems. My thanks also to Nina Koota for deciphering my handwriting and typing the manuscript and to Susan Bein who helped in an emergency.

A very special note of appreciation to my beloved patients who taught me the true meaning of courage, determination and the enjoyment of small achievements.

Contents

The Not-So-Nimble Needlework Book

Introduction

Not so nimble, not so funny. Not being able to thread a needle; not being able to relax doing a piece of needlework; not feeling the exhilaration of creating something with your hands, can be terribly frustrating. Especially to those of us who already have physical problems forcing us to make adjustments in all our daily activities.

During my years as supervisor of Continued Therapy at the Institute for Rehabilitation Medicine at New York University Medical Center, I spent much time planning new and interesting craft projects to stimulate the patients. Most commercial kits were unsuitable for these people so we had to devise, design, and adjust the patterns. The patients found them easier to do; the designs were more original and personal; and the results were rewarding to the instructor as well as the pupil.

So it seems to me that many of the methods and materials we used so successfully at the Institute can benefit a great many more people in the community: those with temporary or permanent ailments due to accident, illness, or aging; the numerous millions with stiff fingers, faulty vision, aches, pains, and sprains—all those everyday miseries that don't really require professional therapy but from which so many of us suffer. Since I, too, am a member of that aching society I decided to investigate the situation more intensively.

I sought information on crafts for people of all ages with ordinary disabilities—permanent or temporary. I went to libraries, public and private institutions, commercial outlets here in the United States and in several foreign countries. There are good technical and professional articles for therapists and

11

teachers. The book and craft shops have an avalanche of beautifully executed volumes on all types of needlecrafts; but they are geared for the agile and talented. There is also a confusing multitude of kits for sale. And after all my research, I discovered that I simply could not find anything specifically designed for the "not-so-nimble." We are left to fend for ourselves—victims of common human frailty—yet we are greatly in need of guidance and advice.

I accept the fact that because of changes in my eyesight, petit point or other minute stitches have become too difficult. I accept the fact that latchet hooking a rug tires my slightly arthritic hands. My patience runs short when a project is too detailed or repetitious. Despite all these changes, I shall not surrender my needles, yarns, and fabrics. And with this book, I hope to encourage you to follow my example. Needlework still gives me rewarding hours and needed relaxation. Instead of becoming frustrated straining to do what I used to do, I am enjoying the new challenge of getting good interesting results with revised methods. My aim in this book is to motivate you to adapt yourself to new approaches and new materials. Using needlework as the means, you can help yourself conquer the dread diseases of boredom, tension, loneliness, and even pain. There is nothing that gives the exhilaration of achievement—planning something, making something, having, giving, or perhaps even selling something that is practical and beautiful.

And, now, let's begin.

1
Fundamentals

I can sympathize with you if you become bored or irritated with everyone who offers you orders or advice in your life. There are so many things we "must" do. So please bear with me while I revert to my teaching days and "strongly suggest" a few simple but cardinal rules to follow in order to maximize your needlework enjoyment. These rules leave no room for compromise if you want to work efficiently and avoid strain and fatigue.

Basic Working Conditions

It would be ideal to set up a work area for yourself or have someone help you do it. You need a chair or a bed with proper support for yourself, good lighting, a work surface, and a container for your supplies. This is not too difficult to arrange in your own home, a recreation room, or hospital room.

You will actually be more alert and have better endurance if you sit in a fairly straight chair such as a dining, bridge, or pull-up chair with arms and padded seat and back. A lounge chair is fine for watching television, taking a nap, or reading, but it is tiring to sit in for needlework since one tends to slump into it. Out bodies sink too deeply into the soft cushion, and our arms are not in proper working position.

A wheelchair is designed for proper sitting. If you require one, you can work sitting in it or, if you prefer, you may transfer to one of the types of chairs described above.

If you are confined to a hospital bed, it is easily adjusted to a sitting position; if you are in an ordinary bed, a few firm pillows at your back, and perhaps one under your knees, is beneficial. A backrest can also support your back. This is a large curved-shaped pillow about 16 inches high and 30 inches from arm to arm, available in a variety of fabrics. I also find a backrest is comfortable when used on a sofa or deep chair during the hours I want to join the family in the living room and work at the same time. Backrests can be purchased in home furnishing shops and departments or through catalogues.

Proper lighting is equally as important as proper seating. Clear bright daylight is the best (use it for matching colors of yarns and fabrics). But since daylight is not always available, you have to substitute a correctly placed lamp. Very few ceiling lights are adequate. If you work right-handed, the light should come from slightly behind on your left. If you work left-handed, the light should be behind you and slightly to the right.

Some of the new high-intensity lights are fine too; but make sure that they cover a large enough area to light up your hands and your work but, at the same time, don't strain your eyes.

The next necessity is a sturdy table or tray of proper height upon which you can rest your materials, your hands, and your lower arms. You may find it more restful to put your elbows on the table while you are working. Your materials should be within your grasp so you don't have to twist or stretch to reach them.

A container is the final requirement. It can be a shopping bag, a hat box, a basket, or a tote bag—preferably one with a handle—to hold all items needed for the project. This serves two purposes. You will avoid the nuisance of searching for mislaid scissors, thread, and pins; and you will make your work portable so that you can move it and work on it as you go from room to room, from one house to another, while waiting for doctors or dentists, and when visiting or traveling. Of course this works better with small-sized projects. I can't count how many granny squares I've crocheted during these times. As a result I have lovely afghans to show instead of frayed nerves.

Good Tools Are a Necessity

Scissors

If your basic tools are of a proper type and good quality, they can help rather than hinder you. Don't waste motion snipping two or three times with dull blades when you can do it once.

Small, sharp-pointed embroidery scissors are a must for cutting yarn and threads. Sharp 8- or 9-inch scissors are good for cutting fabric. The new scissors with contoured handles are very comfortable to use. Left-handed scissors are also available. An ambidextrous snipper, which works like a tweezer with a squeezing action to cut thread, may help if it is difficult for you to use ordinary scissors. Pinking shears are a lovely luxury for cutting fabrics with an edge that doesn't ravel easily. If you want to spend a little more, perhaps you can get electric scissors.

Thimbles

A thimble can be helpful. Even if you have never used one before, try it. It really saves your fingertips when pushing the needle through the fabric. A metal thimble is lighter but a plastic one is almost as good. Make sure that your thimble fits properly; they come in various sizes.

I have also used a rubber finger cover (sold in office supply stores for filing) to protect my index finger from too much friction when working with rough yarns.

Pins

When used efficiently, pins can almost serve as an extra hand. You can use ordinary straight pins, but those with a plastic ball top are easier to see, pick up, and handle. T-pins (named for their shape) are strong and can be used for holding fabric and yarn in place on a frame or board. Make sure that all pins are rustproof and sharp pointed. Discard those that are rough and bent as this will prevent small accidents.

Needles

Many different kinds of needles have been designed for different types of needlework. We shall ignore the very fine ones for they are too difficult for us to use. There is the long-eyed, sharp-pointed shape usually referred to as a crewel, embroidery needle, or cotton darner #5. These come with various sizes of eyes. You may find the ones with the largest eye the best to use for normal sewing, appliqué, simple quilting, and embroidery on tightly woven fabric.

Blunt-pointed needles are used for needlepoint and much of the embroidery in this book. These are called tapestry needles, and I use a #18.

When working on quick point canvas or rug canvas (3–5 holes to an inch) you can use a larger type called a rug needle, or a #13.

Most of these needles are easily available in packages in your needlework or notions store.

The exact type of needle you will need for your project will be listed in the specific instructions.

If you have difficulty in threading a needle, look under Self-Help Aids in this chapter.

Other Tools You May Need

You may or may not need any of the following, but they can come in handy: a measuring tape, a ruler, yardstick, tacks, a hammer, graph paper, tracing paper, pencils, and pens. Specific instructions and equipment are included with each project.

Yarns and Threads

The range of yarn and thread colors and textures has never been as varied as it is today. You can find huge assortments in your local variety store, needlework store, or through catalogues. Start a collection of yarns—even odds and ends—they can all be used.

Remember to buy enough yarn—or perhaps a bit extra—to complete your project as dye lots differ. Most stores will give you a refund or credit for any unopened full packages that you return.

Use good quality yarns. For your larger meshes you will need heavier weights. These are easier to handle, cover the mesh more thoroughly, and generally give a superior appearance. Since you are putting in so much effort, it would be unwise to skimp on quality. This is a good place not to be "pound foolish."

Pick a Project

Before you make a decision—think. First be realistic and recognize your limitations. Select what you can do comfortably—it is usually the right thing; however, if you are not sure, consult your doctor. Don't strain to do what you did formerly or what you would like to do regardless of its effect on your well-being. There is no profit in causing yourself further pain and frustration when you can substitute a sensible, enjoyable experience. If one technique is not suitable, try something else: keep an open mind and get help when you need to do so.

At this point I would like to introduce an invaluable anonymous being to whom we shall refer as the "Helping Hand," who can be a relative, friend, neighbor, or teacher whose assistance you require either to get your materials or start you on your project. You may need someone to do only one line of work to simplify a pattern or show you how to do a new stitch. Don't let this prevent you from becoming involved. It is much wiser to get a Helping Hand than to have false pride and achieve nothing.

Secondly, work on something that gives you satisfaction. There is no point in doing something just to keep busy or just because it's around the house. Try to work on a project that is pleasing: make it a joy, not a chore.

Here are a few questions that may help you decide on your project:

Is it more comfortable for you to do smaller motions such as sewing, needlepoint, or embroidery?

Does repetitive motion such as knitting or crocheting tire you?

Have you previously worked on some of these techniques?

Would you like to learn something new?

Do you want to make something practical, decorative, or both?

Do you need a birthday gift?

Do you have a sick friend who can use some cheering?

Is someone going to have a baby?

Could your room use a bright new accent?

How about gifts for the holidays?

Isn't a tote bag always useful?

Can you use a new belt for a new dress or to spruce up an old one?

Can you use a coverlet or afghan to keep you warm in these fuel-saving days, or a shawl to warm your back?

Would you like some new place mats to entice your eye as well as your palate?

Would you like to save some money?

It can be less expensive and more creative to do it yourself.

Design: Keep It Simple

To begin your project, I would suggest that you follow the directions I have worked out in the following pages. They have all been done with care to aid you. After you feel more secure about your technique, you may want to change some patterns; please feel free to do so.

Best of all, when you feel really brave and proficient, I heartily urge you to work out your own designs. You will find this most rewarding for they will be a product of your own mind and hands—your very own creation. You might even find it valuable to start a collection of pictures and notations for future reference. There have been volumes written on the topic of design; however, I shall list less time-consuming and more readily available sources.

Keep it simple; this does not mean childish or dull. Picasso could draw a human figure with a few lines; a bare tree is a fascinating form; a slice of an orange is a good design; a bunch of flowers is beautiful.

The object of your project should help with your choice.

For whom is it? Yourself, a baby, a teen-ager? What is it for? A living room, a nursery, a kitchen? Something to wear? What do you like? Nature's forms, abstract designs, Indian motifs, or perhaps geometrics?

Sources

Sources surround you. Indeed, you can find ideas wherever you look.

Books and magazines offer boundless suggestions for projects and designs. There are needlework books, art books, children's coloring and story books, gardening books, seed catalogues, home decorating, fashion, and family-type books, and periodicals. You may even find ideas in advertisements.

Fabric prints have never been as varied and exciting as they are now. Just look at the shelves in a fabric store—florals, abstracts, animal prints, patchwork prints. Don't forget the upholstery fabrics, rugs, and household linens. If you find it difficult to shop, check through the home decorating magazines. You may find the form of a flower or a color combination in a print to inspire you.

Wallpaper, gift wrapping paper, and greeting cards are another tremendous source of patterns and color.

Museum reproductions, cards, and slides offer a most artistic selection if you are fortunate enough to have a museum accessible; if not, for a small cost, many museums will mail you catalogues.

Nature has always been the greatest inspiration for artists and craftsmen.

Visualize trees, flowers, birds, fish, fruits, vegetables, stones, mountains, etc. Adopt, adapt, trace, and copy if you choose. Your individuality will be revealed somewhere in your interpretation. The same design can appear different when executed by different people using different colors, yarns, and fabrics.

You can now recognize how many sources of inspiration are readily available. These sources and your imagination should help you enormously, but don't make slavish copies of pictures; put something of yourself into your work.

To Transfer a Pattern

To trace a pattern from this or any other book you can use either tracing paper or the dull side of fine tissue paper. Paper clips placed along the edges of the tracing paper will prevent the paper from slipping. An embroidery transfer pencil is an efficient tool for reproducing the design. Make sure that your pencil has a good point.

Remove your traced drawing from the page. Place it with the penciled side of the paper on the fabric you are using and press down on the design with a warm iron. You may have to press more than once to get a clear transfer. Do not move the iron back and forth as this blurs the image. This is a good method for embroidery projects.

You can also trace a design and transfer it onto a piece of cardboard. The drawn shape is cut out and used as a pattern. The shape may then be placed wherever necessary on the fabric. With a pencil or marking pen, draw around the shape. The advantage of this method is that the cardboard can be used over and over again.

We suggest that you trace designs with simple clear outlines in the exact size needed. Enlarging and reducing sizes is not simple for the not-so-nimble.

Color

Work with colors that please you; but don't be so rigid that you won't experiment. Color can often be used instead of an intricate pattern to achieve interesting effects. Try to mix new combinations. If you've always been partial to pastels, try some bright hues. Use shades of one color for a subtle monochromatic scheme. If you are overly concerned about matching, remember that exquisite bouquets explode with all kinds of color held together by many shades of green. (This is also a great way to use up odd amounts of yarn.) You cannot go wrong if you take a lesson from nature. Be bold with color—it can be an exciting experience and result in dramatic effects.

Size

Work within your limitations. Don't select a project that is too cumbersome to handle or takes a year to finish, for it will become a burden instead of a pleasure. Here I have included a small rug, a large shawl, and an afghan for those of you who prefer to work on a fairly large piece; but I don't recommend anything more time-consuming.

Self-Help Aids

The following suggestions can be most valuable in solving simple but irritating problems. Most of the products are easily obtainable and, with few exceptions, are very reasonably priced.

Needle Threading

- Dipping the tip of your thread or yarn in a bit of glue or rubbing it on a piece of soap will stiffen it for easier manipulation.
- For ordinary sewing you can buy self-threading needles which are made with a slot opening at the top of the eye through which the thread is slipped.
- A simple diamond-shaped wire threader is often enclosed in a needle pack or may be bought individually. The wire point is inserted through the needle eye. The thread is put through the wire loop. The loop with the thread in it is pulled back through the eye, thus threading the needle. Then simply remove the wire threader. The wire threader is also available with a small magnifying glass. In addition, it can be had with a wooden handle which you may find easier to grasp.
- There is a yarn threader shaped like a flat, elongated metal disc with a hole at each end. The larger hole is used for

Yarn threader

heavier yarns; the smaller hole for finer yarns. This works by inserting the yarn in the proper hole and slipping the end of the disc through the needle eye.
- For threading a sewing needle, there is a plastic mechanical device consisting of a holder for the spool of thread, a tube into which you insert the nee-

dle, and a small push button which forces the thread through the needle eye. This can be used with one hand if necessary.

- You can also help yourself put yarn through a needle eye by looping about two inches of yarn across the width of the needle. Pinch the two pieces of yarn together under the needle. Pull the loop back and forth across the needle to flatten the loop. As you gently slide it off the needle keep pinching the fold between your thumb and index finger. Push the eye of the needle down over the folded edge. This sounds complicated, but is very simple once you get the idea.

- This is a very easy way to get yarn threaded: cut a piece of stiff paper (a piece of an envelope will do) about 2 inches long and narrow enough to fit through the needle eye. Fold the

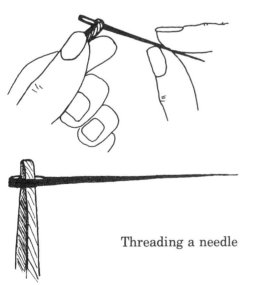

Threading a needle

paper over the tip of the yarn and push it through. You could also use a piece of masking tape and then cut it off before you begin work. This can be done one-handed if you put your needle into a pincushion to keep it upright.

- Again for one-hand use, glue a piece of cork or styrofoam to your working frame or to a heavy wooden block and use this as a needle holder. You can also use a ball of Play-Dough.

- Are you still having trouble? Ask a Helping Hand to thread many lengths of yarn into many needles. Keep them pinned to a piece of felt attached to a wire clothes hanger. The yarns won't tangle and can be easily withdrawn.

Work Supports

Hoops and frames are practical for everyone to use but particularly for the not-so-nimble. *We* need extra support.

Embroidery hoops are familiar to all of you. These consist of two round or oval rings (one fitting closely over the other) made of wood, metal, or plastic. We prefer the wooden type with the adjustable spring and screw as this seems to hold your fabric a little more firmly; however, the others also are suitable. The 8-inch or 10-inch diameter hoop may be the easiest for you to use.

The embroidery hoop can either be held in your hands or attached with a C-clamp to the edge of a table (this keeps your hands free to work). It is advisable to put a towel or cloth underneath the clamp to protect the table.

There is a new type of hoop on a short stand which can be used in two ways. You can either place the hoop's base on a low table or you can sit on the flat base so that you can work with the hoop in your lap. This leaves your hands free to work efficiently. The price for this device, though, is moderately expensive.

Floor frames and inexpensive hoops are lovely luxuries which enable you to work more freely with their firm stands holding your work. Many can also be adjusted to various heights. You can embroider with one hand holding the needle on top of the fabric and the other hand under it to return the needle; or if you have the use of only one hand you can push the needle down from the top, put your hand under the work and push the needle back up.

Another inexpensive frame is the stretcher frame which you can purchase in art supply and some hardware stores. Artists use these frames to hold their canvases for painting, and they come in handy for needle artists as well. You merely staple or tack the needlepoint canvas or embroidery fabric to the frame. The object is to keep the canvas straight and taut. Make sure that you leave enough edge allowance on your canvas to attach it to the frame (2–3 inches on each side should be adequate). Begin your stapling from the top center. Then pull your canvas tightly and staple the bottom center, then the side centers. Keep your canvas straight horizontally and vertically at all times. Next, staple from the centers out to the corners of the canvas so that your staples are about ½ inch apart.

When you have completed attaching your canvas to the stretcher, you are ready to work. We have found that if you lean the upper edge of the frame on a sturdy box or fat telephone directory which has been put on a table, the slanted angle enables you to reach under your project and work with two hands much as you would with the floor or pedestal frame.

You may also find a cork or acoustical tile board helpful, particularly for laying out appliqué patterns. T-pins can be used to hold materials to the boards and will allow you to easily move your cut-out pieces.

Magnifying Lenses

If your eyesight is not as keen as it used to be, there are items to aid (increase) your vision: there are magnifying glasses which you can wear or those which you can clip on to your own lenses. My favorite is a round-framed lens about 4 inches in diameter which is suspended around the neck by an adjustable cord. Rest the shaped frame against your chest so that you see the canvas magnified. This leaves your hands free for work and clearly magnifies your stitches (as well as reading material).

Magnifying lens

Helpful Fabrics and Trimmings

Some of these are old, some are new. All are worthy of your attention. These fabrics provide efficient, simple shortcuts, with the additional benefit of being reasonably priced and easy to find in any notion department of the five and ten.

Easy-Care Fabrics

- Whenever possible use color-fast, shrink-proof, drip-dry, soil-resistant fabrics—anything that lessens extra work is a plus.

- Woven, not printed, plaids and ginghams are best to work with. You can follow the lines for cutting and sewing. Cross Stitch on gingham is easy to do and looks lovely. Try it for place mats.

- Patchwork by the yard lends itself to many projects without the tedious task of sewing small pieces together. It can be re-embroidered, quilted, or used as it is for many projects.

- Printed dolls and animals to cut out, stuff, and sew are sold by the piece. These can be used as sold. And if you prefer to decorate them, you can add beads, laces, and ribbons. You could even turn them into educational toys adding snaps, zippers, ties, and buttons.

- Counted-thread fabrics are easy on the eyes (we use 4–7 holes per inch) and are sold in groups of beautiful colors and textures. These are known as Panama, Herta, and Counted Jute. I recommend the use of contrasting threads for better visibility on these fabrics as well as on all others.

- Use larger-holed, canvas mesh for needlepoint; it is better for your eyes, hands, and nerves.

- New plastic mesh for needlepoint does not pull out of shape, and it works up quickly and beautifully particularly in Bargello patterns. See our tote bag, p. 107.

Ready-Made Trims

- Machine-embroidered motifs—birds, flowers, animals, etc.—can be sewn on individually or can become part of a larger design, mixed with simple embroidery or appliqué for a pillow, wall hanging, or on an article of clothing. Some of these motifs can be ironed on.

- Embroidered flowers, sold by the yard, can be cut apart and used individually as in bouquets combined with hand-embroidered flowers. See our appliquéd wall hanging.

- Fringes and tassels of many styles and colors can be used to finish off or trim pillows, shawls, and wall hangings if you find hand finishing a problem. A circle of fringe with an embroidered center and stem becomes a flower.

- Double-fold braid and wide bias tape can be sewn on needlepoint canvas or woven fabric to make decorative edges and prevent raveling.

- Heavy twisted cords sold by the yard and in many thicknesses and colors can be used for bag handles or sewn on pillows to give them a professional looking finish.

- Lace or crochet doilies can be applied to background fabric for pillows or can be embellished with hand-embroidered flowers or flowers by the yard for new effects as pillows, pictures, or clothing adornment.

Great Connections—Especially Good for the Not-So-Nimble

- Iron-on bonding material is a new product for holding fabrics permanently together without needle and thread. It is available by the yard for fusing large pieces of fabric, or in narrow widths for fastening hems or narrow trims. Place the bonding strips between the two layers of the fabric you wish to join together and steam press. You should follow the manufacturer's directions carefully for proper results. We can use this also to hold trimmings, to interface belts, and to hold appliqués. It is a most versatile and efficient material and saves a great deal of dull hand sewing. This product may be bought under various trade names, such as Stitch Witchery or Polyweb.

- Flexible nylon fabric fasteners are available by the yard, in various widths; or in packaged form in pre-cut shapes for easy attachment to clothing or other materials. This product is easy to apply by gluing, stapling, or sewing; it can be washed or dry-cleaned, and is a superb fastener. And it is much easier to open and close than buttons, snaps, and zippers.

These fasteners have been used extensively in hospitals and are now available to the general public for ordinary use as a closing. They go under the trade names of Velcro, Scotchmate Fabric Fasteners, etc., and may be used for pillow or belt closings, to attach wall hangings to the wall, and to anchor small rugs to prevent slipping.

Keep It Clean

Soil-resistant spray can be used on all work to keep it looking fresh and new. Follow the manufacturer's directions. This product may be purchased under various trade labels, such as Scotchgard.

Hand 2 Sewing

If you are able to grasp and manipulate a sewing needle, hand sewing can be simple yet creative; it can help you decorate your wardrobe and home as well as make attractive gifts. You are the designer. You make the choice of color, fabric, and trim.

Once you have selected your project, collect the equipment needed. In most cases you will have the essentials at home, so there will be no great additional expense. For most sewing you will require:

- needles (large-eyed, pointed-tip crewel, embroidery, or cotton darners #5)
- sewing thread (a shade darker than the fabric will make your stitches less visible)
- sharp scissors
- thimble
- pins (ball-headed, steel, straight pins kept in a pincushion are easiest to handle)
- tape measure, ruler, or yardstick

For greater efficiency, have all your materials ready on a table in front of you. The basic stitches are not difficult to do.

When starting your work, repeat your first stitches two or three times in the same place to secure your thread. End your sewing in the same manner.

Basting is a large, loose running stitch for temporary use in holding seams, hems, appliqués, and in quilting.

The Running Stitch, which is the simplest permanent holding stitch of all,

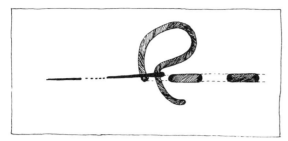

Running Stitch

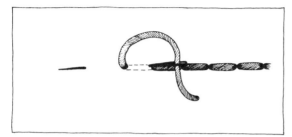

Backstitch

Overcasting is used to hold edges together. This is a slanted stitch, quick and easy to do. We use it for many projects in this book. Hold the two fabric edges together and insert the needle slantwise ¼ inch down from the edges. Try to keep the stitches even in size.

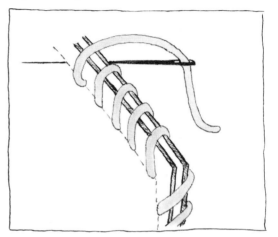

can be used for making seams. You can do a few in and out stitches at one time through your fabric or if you find that too strenuous, you can do one stitch at a time.

Backstitch holds most firmly and is worked as the name implies. Working from right to left, bring needle up and make a small stitch to the right. Bring needle out slightly ahead and to the left of the last stitch. Make your next stitch to the right up to your first stitch. Continue in this fashion.

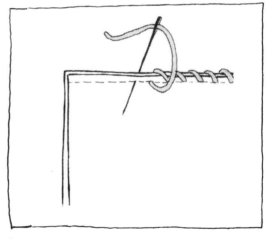

Overcasting

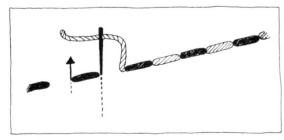

Double Running Stitch

Two rows of Running Stitches one over the other can be used instead of the Backstitch. We call this a Double running stitch.

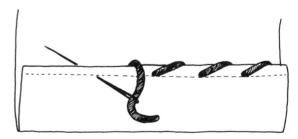

Overcasting a hem

Pins will not only hold your fabric in place but if pinned an even distance from the edge, they will also give you a guide line for stitching.

At this point, we would like to repeat our recommendation to use bonded interfacing and flexible nylon fabric fasteners. We cannot emphasize enough how much these products can simplify your efforts. The bonded interfacing is manufactured in narrow strips in 18-inch widths. It is machine-washable and dry-cleanable and can be used in place of hemming and appliquéing simply by pressing it with a steam iron.

Heating Pad Cover
(finished size 12 inches x 16 inches)

½ yard quilted, washable, cotton print
    fabric (This will make 2 covers)
Needle (crewel or darner #5)
Matching thread
Thimble
Pins
Tape measure

1. Cut the piece of fabric to 14 inches x 18 inches. Fold material in half so that *right* or printed sides are together.

2. Pin and sew the two adjacent sides together about ½ inch in from the edges

(see diagram). Use a Running Stitch, Double Running Stitch, or Backstitch. The third side (top on diagram) is the fold. The fourth side is left open for inserting the heating pad.

3. Turn over a 1-inch hem on this fourth side and secure it either by stitching or pressing on fusible webbing.

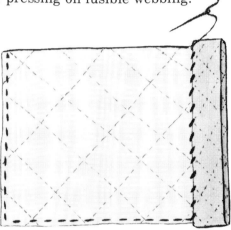

A new heating pad cover can add cheer; a shabby cover can be depressing when you're aching—and it is so simple to make.

Notes and Options

This cover can serve as an attractive and safe cover for a hot water bottle, as well.

Washcloth Pillow
(finished size 12 inches x 12 inches)

2 matching printed washcloths (designer-type)
1½ yards trim, ready-made fringe, ball fringe, or tassels (see directions for tassels)
1 foam pillow form 12 inches x 12 inches or 1 package Dacron fiberfill. One package will fill two pillows.

Washcloth pillows

Embroidery needle
Embroidery floss or matching thread, doubled
Thimble
Pins
Tape measure

1. Place two cloths, wrong sides together.
2. Pin and sew together three of the sides (see diagram). Leave one side open for insertion of the pillow form or stuffing. If you want your stitches to be invisible, use thread which matches the washcloth. If you want the stitches to be part of your trim however, use contrasting, colored embroidery floss which will add interest. You can do a simple Running Stitch, a Double Running Stitch, the Backstitch, or the Blanket Stitch. (See stitch directions, pp. 44–46).

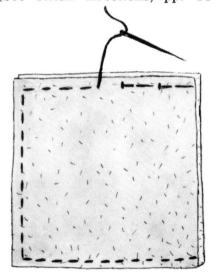

Pin and sew together three of the sides.

Sew your stitches about ¼ inch in from the edges.

3. Insert the pillow form or stuffing.
4. Stretch, pin, and sew the fourth side.
5. You can embellish the pillow by sewing on ready-made or handmade tassels at each corner. (See directions for tassels on p. 152.) You can also stitch on ready-made fringe or ball fringe in a contrasting color.

This little pillow is a lovely, useful, washable, and inexpensive item.

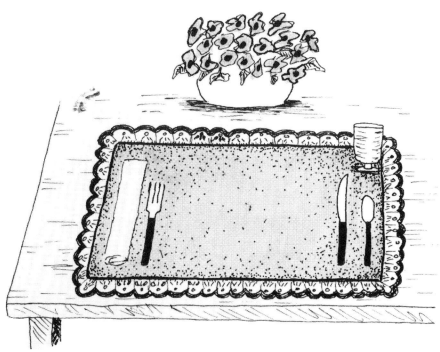

Set of Four Place Mats

1⅛ yards of 36-inch-wide washable fabric
8 yards ruffled eyelet cut into four equal lengths
Embroidery needle
Matching thread
Thimble
Pins
Scissors
Tape measure or ruler

1. Fold the fabric in half; pin the edges and cut on the fold. Cut the two resulting pieces in half again so that you have 4 equal rectangles approximately 18 inches x 20 inches.
2. On each rectangle, right side down, fold back a ¾-inch hem. Pin and stitch the hem with small Running Stitches.
3. Repeat this method on all four sides of the four mats.
4. Pin the heading of the ruffle to the mat hem—wrong sides of both ruffle and hem together. Stitch around each mat and join the two ends of the ruffle neatly.

Notes and Options

These mats are a little larger than usual to insure better table protection as I find most place mats too small.

If you want to do less sewing, you can turn up the hems and use narrow iron-on bonding material to fuse them.

Stitch a Printed Doll

Printed doll fabric
Dacron stuffing
Embroidery needle
Matching thread
Thimble
Pins
Scissors

There are now available in sewing, notion and craft outlets an assortment of doll and animal patterns printed on fabric which you cut out, stitch, and stuff. One of our favorites is a replica of an old-fashioned seated cat. Another is a doll. We have made many of each as

Stitch a printed cat

gifts. We have given the cat to adults, embellishing it with jeweled button eyes and a fancy ribbon bow tie. For children, we omit the hazardous button eyes and tie a yarn collar with a securely knotted bell around the neck.

The stuffed doll can be given as is. For an older child, however, it may be decorated to become an educational toy by the addition of buttons and loops or laces sewn on the printed shoes or snap fastenings stitched to a small apron. This can be a gift to teach small fingers to button, tie bows, and open and close snaps.

Bouncing frog

Bouncing Frog or Butterfly

7-inch x 7-inch piece of dark green felt
7-inch x 7-inch piece of light green felt
7-inch x 7-inch piece of printed fabric
Dacron stuffing
¾ yard white round elastic (millinery elastic)
Sewing needle
Matching thread
Thimble
Pins
Scissors
Tape measure
Tracing paper
Hot-iron transfer pencil

1. Trace the pattern of the frog's body onto tracing paper with a hot-iron transfer pencil. Transfer the traced pattern by pressing it with a warm iron onto the two appropriate fabrics (the top of the body on the print, the underbody on the felt fabric). Cut out the shapes. Trace the frog's legs on tracing paper, transfer them to the green felt and cut out the shapes.
2. Right sides together, pin and stitch the print material to the dark green felt body, using a Backstitch; leave opening at head. Turn inside out.
3. Stuff tightly with Dacron stuffing and sew up opening, using an Overcasting Stitch.
4. Place legs on body, according to the sketch. Pin and stitch in place with a Running Stitch or Backstitch.
5. Eyes can be put on with an indelible marking pen. Buttons are not recommended if this is to be a child's toy.
6. Make a loop of the elastic by knotting the two ends in a square knot. Sew the looped elastic piece to the middle of the body on the printed fabric. The knotted loop of the elastic is the handle.

Notes and Options

We have included a pattern for a butterfly for you to use if you prefer it to the frog. The method of putting it together is the same.

The top and bottom may be made of two different colors of felt also.

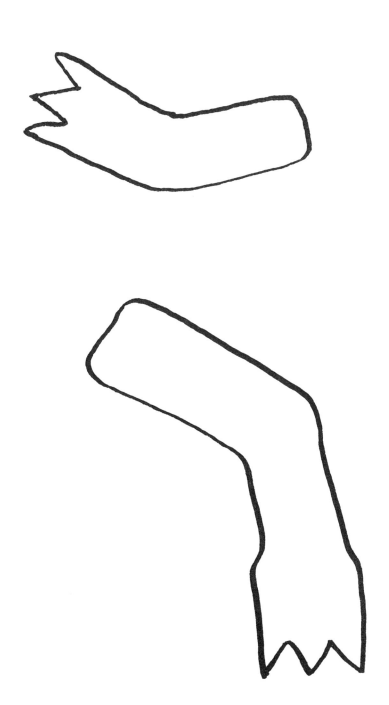

Frog pattern—make two of each piece.

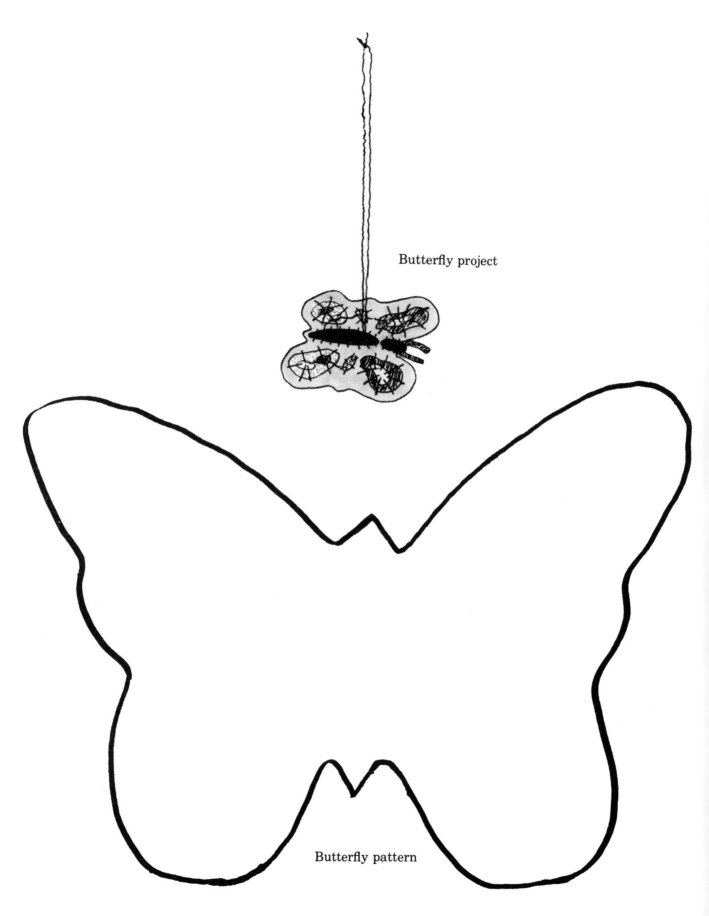

Butterfly project

Butterfly pattern

Bedside holder

Bedside Holder

½ yard 40-inch-wide washable heavy cotton or quilted fabric

8½-inch x 13¾-inch piece of shirt cardboard

1½ yards lace or ribbon trimming

Embroidery needle

Matching thread

Thimble

Pins

Scissors

Tape measure or ruler

1. Lay the fabric right side down and cut it to measure 16 inches x 40 inches.
2. Fold back a 1-inch hem on all four sides. Pin and sew the hem using a small Running Stitch or Backstitch.
3. On the narrow end of the fabric, fold over a 9-inch casing and pin across only. Leave the sides open for inserting the cardboard. (The board can also be removed for washing the hold-

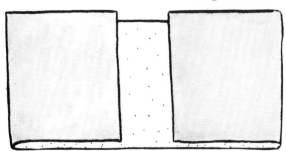

Fold over the fabric.

er.) Sew the pinned seam, using a small Running Stitch or Backstitch. This section is slipped between the box spring and mattress to secure the holder.

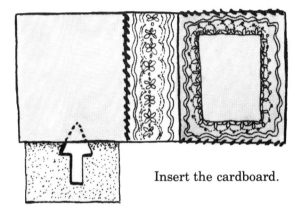

Insert the cardboard.

4. Turn the other narrow end of your fabric up 10 inches for the pocket. Here you pin and stitch only the side seams together.
5. Pin the lace or ribbon around the edge of the pocket and stitch it in place.

Notes and Options

Decorate the pocket portion only. You can divide the pocket in sections by doing a row of vertical stitches through both thicknesses of fabric. This is a convenient holder for eyeglasses, pills, books, and tissues.

Cylinder Bolster Cover

23-inch x 26-inch piece of fabric (prefer-
    ably washable)

1 yard of 2-inch-wide fringe cut into 2
    equal pieces

2 yards of rug yarn, cording or ¼-
    inch-wide ribbon cut into 2 equal
    pieces

18-inch x 20-inch cylinder pillow form
    with Dacron stuffing

Embroidery needle

Matching thread

Thimble

Pins

Scissors

Tape measure or ruler

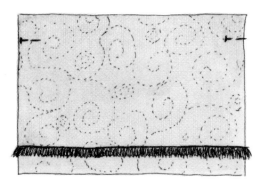

Fringe placement

1. Lay the fabric flat, right side up, the
   longer side facing you.
2. Measure 5 inches in from both sides
   and mark the top and bottom with
   pins to indicate the placement of the
   fringe.
3. Place and pin the fringe heading

along this line, remembering that
the open fringe ends face out to the
fabric edge.

4. Stitch the trim to the fabric with a
   small Running Stitch or Backstitch.
5. Turn the piece wrong side up.
6. Fold back a 1½-inch hem on each
   narrow end. Pin and stitch down.

7. On the two long sides you are going
   to make a casing for the ribbon pulls

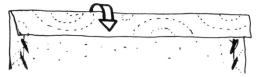

Casings on the long sides

by turning back a ¾-inch hem and
then turning it back again for
¾ inch to make a neater stronger
casing. Pin and stitch.

8. Pull the ribbon through the casing
   (leaving a 6-inch tail) by attaching a
   medium-sized safety pin to the end

Hems on the short sides

of the ribbon and forcing the pin through the casing; the ribbon will

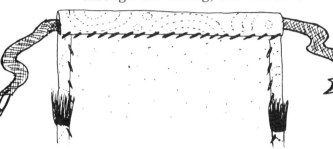

Ribbon pulled through casing

trail after it. Remove the pin after the ribbon has emerged.

9. Place the pillow form in the center of the cover and roll the fabric snugly around it.
10. At each side, pull the two ribbon ends tightly to gather the edges and tie them into a bow.

Notes and Options

Lace ruffles or ribbon can be used for trim.

Floral print fabrics will camouflage uneven stitches.

The lines of woven gingham can be used as guides for hem lines and stitches.

This is a particularly comfortable pillow for supporting your head. It can also relax your legs by placing it under your knees when you are lying in bed.

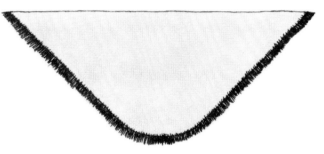

Cape Shawl

1½ yards 54-inch-wide jersey (the width of your fabric determines the size of the finished shawl)
3 yards ready-made fringe
Embroidery needle
Matching thread
Thimble
Pins
Scissors

1. Place the fabric on a table and fold it in half diagonally, right sides together, and pin to hold in place.

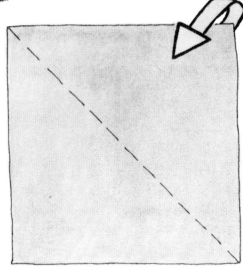

Fold fabric diagonally.

2. Fold the fabric in half again, open sides to open sides. Pin along edge to hold.

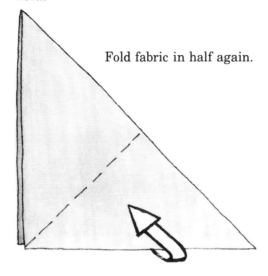

Fold fabric in half again.

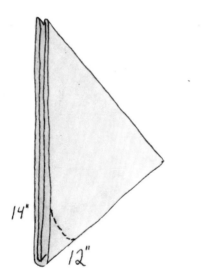

Mark for bottom curve.

14"
12"

3. Measure 12 inches up from the bottom point and mark with a pin.

4. Measure 14 inches along the open sides and mark with another pin.

5. Take your scissors and cut a curve from the 12-inch mark to the 14-inch mark.

6. Unpin and unfold to the original triangle (the shawl now has a graceful curved bottom).

7. Sew the open edges together using small Running Stitches or Back-stitches. Leave a 6-inch opening to allow for turning the cape inside out to the right side.

8. Turn and stitch up the opening.

9. Attach the heading of the fringe about 1 inch above the seamed edge. Pin and stitch. Don't forget to tuck under the cut ends of the fringe heading for a neater finish.

Notes and Options

You can use ruffled edging, heavy crochet lace, or a band of embroidered ribbon for trim. These may be sewn on or fused on by using iron-on bonding strips.

This shawl can be made in wool jersey for cool climate or synthetic jersey for warmer areas.

If you are really ambitious, you can do a Blanket Stitch around the hem edge and add handmade fringe.

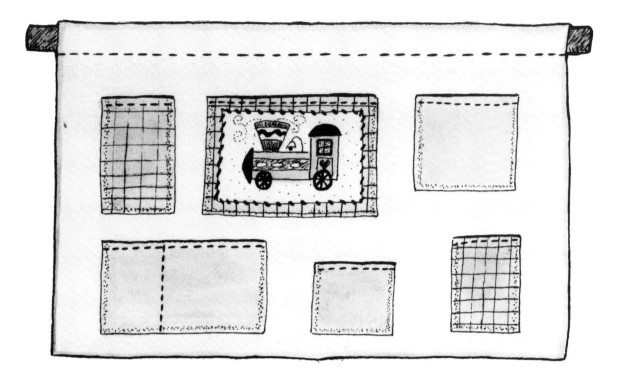

Pocket Wall Hanging

⅔ yard red felt

Small pieces of gingham for pockets (Actually these can be any size depending upon your purpose.)

green: 4 inches x 7 inches
yellow: 5½ inches x 4¾ inches
turquoise: 13½ inches x 7 inches
red: 8 inches x 7½ inches
yellow print: 7½ inches x 8½ inches
navy: 8¾ inches x 7¾ inches

4 yards narrow iron-on bonding strips

1 yardstick, dowel, or curtain rod 36 inches long for hanging

Embroidery needle

Thread

Thimble

Pins

Scissors

Tape measure or ruler

1. With your felt flat on a table, wide side in front of you, fold a 2-inch hem to form the casing for the hanging rod. Leave the ends open. Pin and sew hem with a Double Running Stitch or Backstitch.

2. Turn your felt to the right side and arrange your gingham squares on the felt in a pleasing design. Pin them onto the felt only.

3. As you work, remove each pocket individually.

4. Turn under a 1-inch hem on four sides and press them flat. You can use

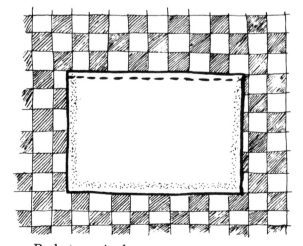

Pocket on gingham

the lines of the gingham as guides. Pin and stitch the top hem only.

5. Replace the pocket to its original position and secure it with pins in the center. Leave the bottom and side edges free.

6. Cut your iron-on bonding strips into three pieces to fit under these three sides.

7. Press your pocket edges to the felt with the bonding strip between them. Follow the manufacturer's directions for the type of bonding strip you have selected.

8. Repeat this process for each pocket.

9. You can section a long pocket by stitching a vertical line through both thicknesses of fabric.

Notes and Options

This is a practical and decorative storage idea which can be varied in size, shape, and trim for many uses.

To further simplify this project, you can make the pockets of varicolored felt which will eliminate all hems.

The pockets can be appliquéd or embroidered, for additional decoration. The holder can be glued, fused, or stapled to a piece of polystyrene or heavy cardboard in order for it to hold heavier weights.

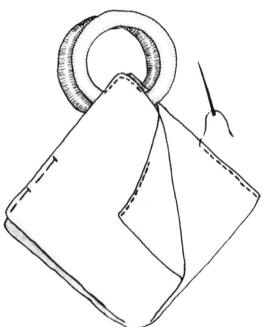

Reversible Kerchief Bag

22-inch-square red-and-white printed bandanna

23-inch x 23-inch piece of blue denim

2 plastic bangle bracelets (red, white, or blue)

Needle
Thread
Thimble
Pins
Scissors
Tape measure

1. Lay the bandanna right side down on the table. Place the blue denim wrong side down over it.
2. Turn a 1-inch hem of denim under the bandanna and pin the edges of the denim to the bandanna.

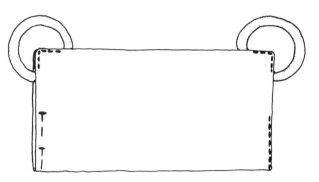

Insertion of bangles and side seams

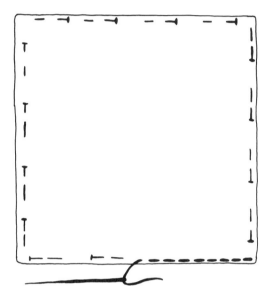

Stitch two squares together.

3. Stitch the denim and bandanna hems together using a small Running Stitch or Overcasting Stitch.
4. Place sewn pieces flat on the table. Fold them in half with the fold at the bottom. Where the upper left-hand corners meet, insert the bangle be- tween the front and back piece 1 inch down from the pointed corner. (You should have two small triangles of fabric, protruding into the center of the bangle.) Pin and sew the sides of this triangle about 1 inch on each side of the point. Repeat this proce- dure on the other corner of the bag with the second bangle. At both ends, sew up 4 inches from the fold. Hold the bracelets together and two points will form. Sew these points as you sewed the sides—4 inches up from the folded bottom.

Notes and Options

Bandannas come in many new colors so that you can vary the look. Of course you may use any other kind of print as well.

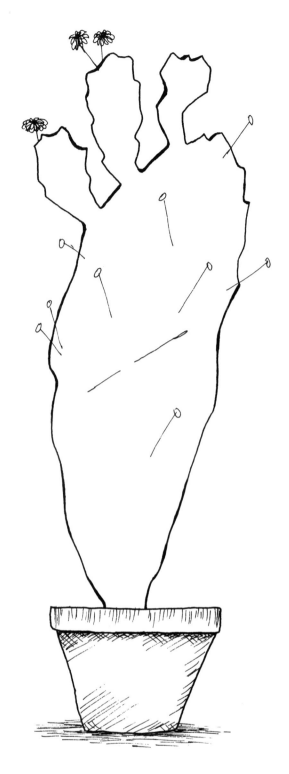

Cactus Pincushion

6-inch x 7-inch piece of green felt
3-inch diameter plastic flowerpot
Small amount of Dacron stuffing

½-inch diameter wooden dowel, 6 inches long
Sand, pebbles, or styrofoam to fill the pot

A few brightly colored straw flowers
Crewel needle
Green sewing thread or embroidery floss
 split into 2 strands
Thimble
Pins
Scissors (pinking shears can add a more
 decorative edge)
Tracing paper
Transfer pencil (the iron-on type is
 easiest)

1. With a transfer pencil, trace the pattern of the cactus from our sketch on to tracing paper.
2. Fold the piece of felt in half to measure 3 inches x 7 inches and pin around the edges to hold it in place.
3. Transfer the tracing to the folded felt fabric and cut out the shapes.
4. With wrong sides together, pin along the edges of the felt leaving an opening at the top of the plant "offshoots" and at the base of the cactus for stuffing. Using a Backstitch, stitch where you have pinned.
5. Insert stuffing in the "offshoots" and stitch this end closed. Insert stuffing through the base into the cactus until it is firmly packed.
6. Insert the dowel into the cactus leaving 3 inches extending at the base for the "stem."
7. Fill the planting pot with sand or pebbles and "plant" your cactus.
8. Insert a few straw flowers into the spaces between stitches at the top of the "offshoots."
9. Colored straight pins can be stuck into the pincushion for a decorative effect.

Notes and Options

Colored felt flowers may be used instead of straw flowers.

This is a practical gift for a hospital patient as it needs no care.

Pillow

Pillow Forms

Ready-made pillow forms of different sizes and shapes can be purchased at most department stores or upholstery shops. We prefer the muslin-covered fiberfill forms as they are washable, lightweight, and remain fluffy and soft. They cost more, but they are worth it. You may satisfactorily use foam rubber forms as well; kapok filling tends to get lumpy.

If you prefer to make your own form, you will need 2 pieces of cotton cloth (usually white) cut 1 inch larger in the width and in the length than your final form. (If you want a 12-inch x 12-inch form, cut your fabric 13 inches x 13 inches.) Place the fabric pieces together, one over the other, and pin around 1 inch in from the edges on three sides and all of the fourth side except for 6 inches in the center for stuffing (closing your four corners gives you a neater form than if you left a corner open until the end). Do a Double Running Stitch or

Backstitch where you have pinned. Turn the case inside out and stuff it with fiberfill. (Shredded foam rubber is very difficult to use.) Make sure that all four corners are well filled. Pin and stitch the opening.

Pillow Covers

Place the 2 pieces of your cover fabric right sides together, and pin them about 1 inch in from the edges around three sides. On the fourth side, continue pinning for 1 inch in from each corner. Stitch where you have pinned. Following the pins do a Double Running Stitch or Backstitch, using matching thread. Turn the cover inside out to the right side. Push out corners from inside with the eraser end of a pencil. Insert your pillow form, filling the corners well. Close the remainder of the fourth side by first pinning the turned under edges together and then stitching as neatly as you can.

You can camouflage uneven stitches and seams with decorative cording, sewn around the border.

Tassels at each corner are another good trimming.

3
Embroidery

Embroidery is an age-old universal craft which gives most satisfying rewards for only a small investment. It requires a few tools: needles, a small, sharply pointed scissors, a thimble; and also, when needed, a hoop or frame, ruler or tape measure, and pins.

Your personal taste and the purpose of your project determine the choice of background material and the appropriate type of yarn or floss.

For your first attempt, follow our designs and suggestions; but as you become more familiar with this medium we hope you will become more original. Here are a few general comments.

Needles

Use long, sharply pointed embroidery or crewel needles with the largest eye possible for easier threading when you embroider on ordinary fabric.

For counted-thread fabrics, use blunt, large-eyed tapestry or chenille needles.

Threads and Yarns

The threads we have used for our patterns are 6-strand cotton floss, perlé (a silky, twisted cotton), and crochet thread. You can also use all weights and textures of wool and orlon. All of these threads are made in a multitude of colors, solid, ombré, and variegated.

When embroidering, use 16- to 18-inch lengths of yarn to prevent arm fatigue as well as tangles. You can save time and effort by threading a few needles and hanging them nearby to keep them untangled. (The idea is to keep the thread hanging vertically to prevent snarling.) It is easier on the eyes if you use darker threads on lighter backing or lighter threads on darker backing.

Fabrics

The ideal backgrounds for the not-so-nimble are the evenly spaced, counted-thread fabrics known as Panama, Herta,

43

or Binca cloth. These are available in a great variety of weaves, textures, and colors. There are also heavier jute types suitable for embroidered rugs. These beautiful backgrounds are worth the additional cost as they do not have to be completely covered with stitches. The weave provides spaces between the threads that can easily be counted and worked without strain. The cloth can be decorated with many simple stitches, and all types of yarn. A blunt size 13 or 18 tapestry needle is easily threaded and penetrates the holes effortlessly.

For other projects use the more loosely woven linen-type materials. Remember that woven checks and stripes can also provide a guide for accurate stitching. Re-embroidering clearly defined printed cloth such as a floral slipcover material can result in a dramatic design. Just following the outlines with either a matching or contrasting thread or yarn and a simple plain or Whipped Running Stitch can work up into an original pillow or tote bag.

Beware of tightly woven, glazed fabrics as they are difficult to pierce with an embroidery needle.

Hoops

When using hoops for certain projects you may have to call on your Helping Hand to stretch your fabric taut and tighten the screws. This embroidery aid keeps your stitches from puckering in addition to holding your work securely.

Starting and Finishing

To start your embroidery, go over your first stitch two or three times to make it hold. To finish off your embroidery, weave through a few worked stitches on the wrong side.

Stitching

Proper embroidery technique is stitching in two steps: If you are right-handed, your right hand pushes the needle down from the top. Your left hand should be under your work to catch the needle and then push it back up through the fabric. NOTE: If you are left-handed, reverse the positions of your hands—left hand on top, right hand underneath.

If you have a weak hand, this two-step method can still be done with one hand doing the two steps. An in-and-out motion in one step results in uneven stitches and tired hands.

Embroidery Stitches

The Running Stitch is the simplest of all stitches; yet it lends itself to many diversified patterns. It can be used for straight or curved outlines or it can be

Running Stitch

used to fill in an area. The stitches can be done in straight even rows or alternated to give a basket-weave look. Interesting combinations can be formed by the use of different weights and colors of yarn. More intricate effects can result from whipping or weaving through the basic Running Stitch using a blunt nee-

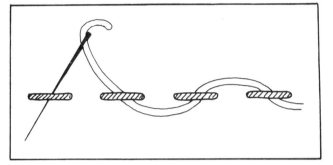

Whipped Running Stitch

dle and contrasting thread. The Whipped Running Stitch resembles the Outline Stitch and may be easier for you to do.

Straight Stitch is exactly what the name describes. It can be used in rows, radiating from a center, or arranged in

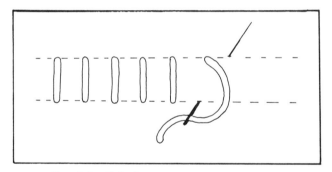

Straight Stitch

groups of three and bound across the center with a horizontal stitch to form a sheaf.

Outline Stitch may be used instead of the Whipped Running Stitch. It does require a bit more control; but works up quickly and clearly.

Cross Stitch is another easy-to-do technique which can be varied by changing the length and width of the stitch.

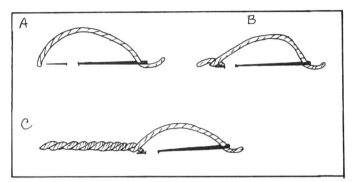

Outline Stitch

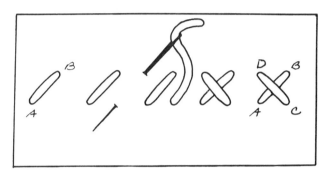

Cross Stitch

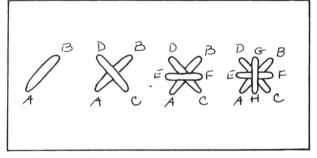

Double Cross Stitch

The cross may be made over a Running Stitch of a contrasting color. To obtain a flower or star shape make a *Double Cross Stitch* which is simply two Cross Stitches, one straight and one diagonal, worked one over the other. We recommend the use of counted-thread fabrics or woven, gingham-checked fabrics on which to work this stitch. You can work in whichever direction is comfortable for you; but remember that all your stitches must cross in the same direction. You can complete one stitch at a time or you can do a row of Half Cross Stitches and then reverse direction and stitch the other Half Cross to complete your row.

The Split Stitch resembles the *Chain-Stitch but* you may find it easier

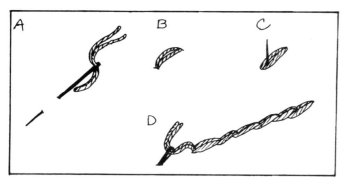

Split Stitch

to do. For best results use 6-strand embroidery floss or yarn doubled.

The Chain Stitch too, requires the use of two hands. It is attractive and works up quickly for outlining or filling in areas.

Chain Stitch

The Buttonhole or *Blanket Stitch* is a lovely edging stitch but it does require the use of both hands. As you work with

Buttonhole or Blanket Stitch

your right hand, your left thumb holds the thread in place. If you are able to do this, you will enjoy doing this stitch. Draw two parallel lines as stitch guides. Work from left to right, bring your needle up at A (which is your lower traced line). Go down to B holding the floss with your left thumb and come up at C. The needle should finish above the thread you are holding. Continue across the row.

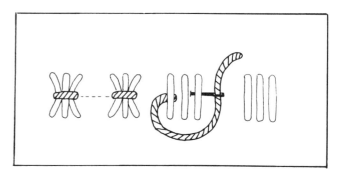

Sheaf Stitch

The Sheaf Stitch consists of three vertical Straight Stitches held together across the center with a Backstitch.

Mirror Mat on Counted-Thread Fabric

9-inch x 11-inch piece of Panama fabric (Herta)
Embroidery floss, 1 skein each:

color A (purple)
color B (red)
color C (green)

Purse mirror
Tapestry needle
Sewing thread of matching color
Thimble
Pins
Scissors
Tape measure
Elmer's glue

1. Cut the fabric to measure 9 inches x 11 inches.
2. Place it right side down and turn under a ½-inch hem; first the long sides then the short sides.
3. Pin the hems in place, lining up the fabric layers so the holes match.
4. With matching thread doubled, sew your hems using a Running Stitch.
5. Turn the mat right side up.
6. Start your embroidery one row in from the edge of the fabric, using color A, and do a Cross Stitch around all four sides of the piece.
7. Using color B, work Cross Stitches in the row below color A, and again around all four sides.

8. Using color C, work Cross Stitches in the row below color B and around all sides. This gives you the border.
9. Find the center of the piece, place the mirror over the center so that you have an equal number of holes on either side and the same number of holes from the bottom and the top.
10. Mark off the outline of the mirror and embroider the first row of Cross Stitches around the mirror. This will vary since purse mirrors come in different sizes.
11. Continue the design outward until completed. I used three rows of Cross Stitches in color A, B, and C to frame the mirror. The words and flowers are optional.
12. Place Elmer's glue on the mirror back, press firmly in place, and put a heavy weight on the mirror. Leave the weight on the mirror overnight.
13. The mat and mirror should fit into a ready-made frame.

Quick-Trim Embroidery

With a few simple stitches you can create a very personal trimming which can change the ordinary into something special. Here are a few suggestions.

For an Infant

Decorate an undershirt. For a girl, use pastel, washable cotton floss and embroider a Blanket Stitch around the neck and at the bottom of the sleeves. A few Double Cross Stitch flowers can also be added. For a boy, do a Running Stitch in red and whip it with blue floss. Add a row of Cross Stitches.

For a Teen-ager

Embroider a T-shirt using bolder colors and larger stitches. You can also embroider denim patches which can be purchased in packages in most notion departments. If they are too small for you to hold, pin the patch to a thin piece of fabric held in an embroidery hoop.

(These patches have a glue-like back and the needle will have to be pushed through with your thimble—so keep the design simple.)

For Children and Adults

Trim a sweater with a row of Cross Stitches or Blanket Stitches around the neck and cuffs.

You can add your personal touch to knit gloves, mittens, hats, and scarves as well as place mats, aprons, and even curtains. Practice the stitches we have shown on our sampler and select the ones you like the best.

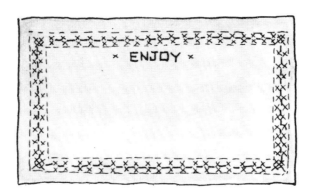

Place Mats on Counted-Thread Fabric
(finished size 12 inches x 17 inches)

1 yard 51-inch-wide Panama or Herta fabric (7 holes to 1 inch)
Embroidery floss or perlé thread:
    1 skein color A (medium blue)
    2 skeins color B (bright orange)
    1 skein color C (olive green)
Tapestry needle
Thread to match fabric
Thimble
Pins

Scissors
Tape measure
Hoop or frame optional (see frame information)

1. Cut your fabric into four pieces, each to measure 13 inches x 18 inches.
2. Place one piece, right side down and turn under a ½-inch hem. Do the long sides first and then the short sides.
3. Pin the hems in place, lining up the fabric layers so the holes match.

4. With matching thread doubled, sew your hems with a Running Stitch or Backstitch.

5. Turn the mat right side up for embroidering.

6. Measure in ¾ inch from the top and ¾ inch from the right side to begin your border. Mark off all corners in the same way.

7. Begin the Running Stitch with color A and embroider around all four sides.

8. Follow the chart for the stitch and color guide.

9. Repeat the procedure on all mats.

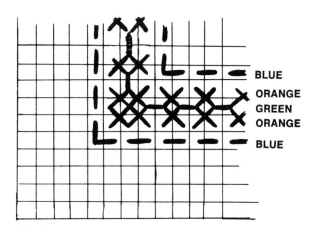

Stitch pattern

BLUE
ORANGE
GREEN
ORANGE
BLUE

Notes and Options

You can vary the stitches and color to suit your own taste.

Any excess fabric can be used for a table runner, mirror mat, or an eyeglass case.

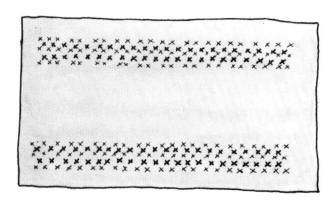

Cross Stitch on Gingham Place Mats
(finished size 12 inches x 16 inches)

1 yard blue-and-white woven gingham
Embroidery floss (split into 3 strands), 1 skein each:
color A (hot pink)
color B (white)
color C (green)
7 yards of ¾-inch iron-on bonding tape
Embroidery needle

50

Thimble
Pins
Scissors
Tape measure
10-inch embroidery hoop (optional)

1. Cut the gingham into four pieces each measuring 14 inches x 18 inches.
2. Place one piece right side down and turn under a 1-inch hem; do the long sides first and then the short sides.
3. Pin the hems in place and baste them.
4. Remove the pins and insert your fabric, right side up, into the embroidery hoop. (If you are better able to work without a hoop, you can omit this step and finish the hem.)
5. Measure in 1 inch from the top and 1 inch from the left side and begin your Cross Stitch. We used hot pink floss for color A on the light blue squares across the top row to within 1 inch of the right side of the mat.
6. Skip 1 row, change to color B floss (we used white) and do the Cross Stitch in the navy squares keeping the margin on the right.
7. In the next row, change to color C (we used green) and do the Cross Stitch in the white squares.
8. In the next row, repeat the white floss in the navy squares.
9. Skip 1 row and repeat color A in the light blue squares.
10. Turn the mat around and repeat the pattern on the opposite side.

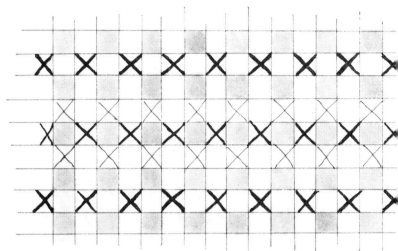

Stitch pattern

11. Measure off and cut two 12-inch and two 17-inch strips of iron-on bonding tape for the hems of the mat.
12. Remove the hoop and turn the mat right side down.
13. Working on one side at a time remove the basting and insert the bonding tape under the hem and press according to the manufacturer's directions.
14. Repeat the entire procedure for the remaining mats.

Notes and Options

The hem is not bonded until the embroidery is completed as the tension of the hoop pulls the bonded hem open.

If you prefer sewing your hem instead of bonding it, turn under a ½-inch hem and then turn it under a second time before stitching. You can do this before you start your embroidery.

"Picasso" Owl on Felt

7-inch x 9-inch piece of white or light-
   colored felt
1 skein black embroidery floss (split into
   3 strands)
Crewel needle

Thimble
Scissors
8-inch embroidery hoop (optional)
Tracing paper
Tracing pencil

1. Trace the simple outline of the pattern and transfer it to the felt piece.
2. Place the felt in the hoop for embroidering.
3. With your split black floss, do a small Running Stitch around all drawn lines.
4. With black floss, whip through all the Running Stitches to give a heavier, clearer outline.

5. This picture can be placed in a 7-inch x 9-inch frame.

Notes and Options

This owl can also be worked and framed in an embroidery hoop by getting the basic piece of felt 9 inches square for an 8-inch hoop or 11 inches square for a 10-inch hoop.

Sun in a Hoop

11-inch x 11-inch square of medium blue linenlike fabric
3½-inch circle of yellow felt
1 skein golden yellow perlé or cotton floss
1 skein black embroidery floss (split into 3 strands)

Crewel needle
Thimble
Pins
Scissors
Tape measure
10-inch embroidery hoop
Drinking glass or other object 3½–4

Sun pattern

inches in diameter to trace the felt circle for the sun's face.

Tracing paper
Tracing pencil

1. Place the fabric, right side up, in the embroidery hoop. Make sure that the fabric is taut and the screw on the outer ring of the hoop is tightly closed. (The hoop will be the permanent frame of this hanging.)
2. Trace a circle onto the felt piece with a pencil and cut out the round shape.
3. Trace the sun face from our pattern onto the felt circle; or draw your own.
4. Place the felt circle in the center of the fabric on the hoop and pin it around the edges.
5. With the black embroidery floss, do a small Running Stitch around the sun's features. Still using black floss, whip stitch through the Running Stitch to give a more solid outline.
6. With gold perlé begin to embroider the sun's rays radiating from the outer edge of the felt face to the inside edge of the hoop using a simple Straight Stitch.
7. When you have finished the long rays, work a radiating row of shorter stitches between the long rays with gold perlé thread.
8. Trim off all the excess linen showing outside of the hoop rim.
9. Tie a looped cord or ribbon to the screw mechanism of the hoop, so the sun can be hung.

Notes and Options

If you wish, you can add colored tape to decorate the hoop frame.

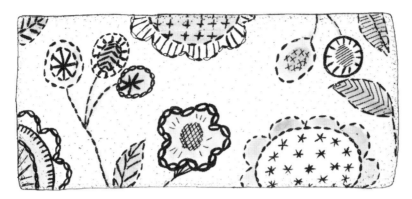

Reembroidered Crewel Print Pillow

24-inch x 20-inch piece of "crewel" print linenlike fabric (This type of cloth is a print of authentic crewel embroidery design and is a perfect base for reembroidery. While the original stitch used was the Chain Stitch, any combination of those shown in the embroidery directions is suitable for a personal decorative expression.)

Embroidery floss, perlé, any lightweight wool or orlon yarn of colors to match the colors in the print.

Pillow form 10 inches x 18 inches

Crewel embroidery needle

Sewing thread (to match background color)

Thimble

Pins

Scissors

Tape measure

Embroidery hoop (optional)

1. Place the fabric, right side up, in the hoop.
2. Select a related color of yarn and begin overstitching the outlines of the print. You can do a Running, Whipped Running, or Chain Stitch to outline the petals of the flowers, the stems, and the leaves.
3. If you wish to fill in the flower centers, you can use a Double Cross Stitch surrounded by a circle of Running Stitches. The flower petals can be filled in with radiating random Straight Stitches of one or two shades. The stems can be worked in Chain Stitch or Whipped Running Stitch. Try using a contrasting yarn such as turquoise to whip through a green Running Stitch for a different effect.
4. When you have reembroidered to suit your own taste, remove the fabric from the hoop and place it, right side up on the table.
5. Fold the fabric in half so that it now measures 12 inches x 20 inches.
6. Complete the pillow following our pillow directions (pp. 41–42).

Notes and Options

This can be a most pleasant project as you can decide how much you wish to reembroider—a few outlines or the entire print. Either way, however, the pillow will be attractive.

This pillow may be further embellished by the addition of twisted cord around the sides or tassels at the four corners.

Any other linenlike fabric with clearly defined flowers will work up almost as well.

Tablecloth on Counted-Thread Fabric

(finished size 43 inches x 43 inches)

1¼ yards of green Panama or Herta fabric cut to 45 inches x 45 inches
#5 perlé floss (53-yard ball) 1 ball each:
   deep orange
   medium orange
   gold
(Embroidery floss may be substituted.)
#18 tapestry needle

Matching green sewing thread for hems
Thimble
Pins
Scissors
Tape measure

1. On the wrong side of the fabric turn under a ½-inch hem and again turn this under ½-inch, lining up the

holes in the layers of fabric as carefully as you can. Pin the hem in place.

2. With matching thread, doubled, sew up the hems with a Running Stitch, Double Running Stitch, or Backstitch. If you insert the needle through the holes of the fabric it will be easier on your hands.

3. Locate the center of the cloth for the center motif by folding the fabric in half horizontally, then folding it in half vertically and mark the spot with a washable marker (a piece of chalk will do).

4. The first block of pattern is made up of 5 rows of medium orange Cross Stitch (the center of this block is the center point of the tablecloth).

5. The easiest way to follow the pattern is from the center out; thus the next motif is 1 row of gold Cross Stitches around the first orange square.

6. Skip over 1 row of fabric holes and leave it unworked around the gold square. Continue the Cross Stitch

square in the next row with gold floss.

7. Do a Straight Stitch (radiating from the center) starting at the corners of each preceding Cross Stitch, skipping over 1 blank hole and ending in the 3rd hole.

8. Skip over 2 rows of fabric holes and leave them unworked. Continue the Cross Stitch using deep orange floss around the square.

9. Repeat the Straight Stitches as before, spanning 3 holes. This completes the center pattern.

10. For the border pattern, measure 5½ inches from the top edge, and 5½ inches in from the left side edge and mark them to begin the Cross Stitch outline. Repeat these measurements at each corner. You will work 1 row of deep orange Cross Stitches completely around the tablecloth.

11. Going from this row inward toward the center, skip over 2 unworked rows of fabric holes and work 1 row of gold Cross Stitches around the cloth.

12. Work 1 row of gold Straight Stitches,

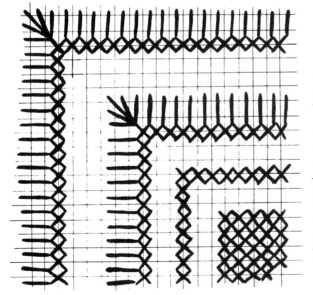

Stitch pattern for center

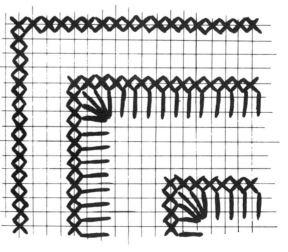

Stitch pattern for border

spanning an empty hole, from the edges of the Cross Stitches so the lines point in toward the center.

13. Skip over 3 unworked rows of fabric holes. With deep orange floss, do 1 more row of Cross Stitches all around the cloth.

14. Work 1 row of Straight Stitches pointing in toward the center.

Notes and Options

You can add a tassel at each corner (See p. 152).

You can vary the colors and stitches to suit your own taste.

Starflower Pillow

15-inch x 15-inch piece of Panama or Herta fabric, 7 holes to 1 inch

15-inch x 15-inch piece of coordinated color fabric for pillow back

4-ply Orlon yarn:
    14 yards color A (terra cotta or rust)
    10 yards color B (olive green)
    6 yards color C (gold)

5 yards color D (yellow)
1 yard color E (brown)
Dacron stuffing or 14-inch square pillow form
#18 tapestry needle
Crewel needle for sewing
Sewing thread to match fabric for pillow back

Stitch pattern

Color key

✕	RUST	A
✗	GREEN	B
✕	GOLD	C
✕	YELLOW	D
✕	BROWN	E

Pins
Thimble
Scissors
Tape measure
Embroidery hoop 10 inches or 12 inches
(optional)

1. This pattern is worked from the center of the flower out. Fold the counted-thread fabric in half vertically; fold it in half horizontally and mark the center spot with a washable marker.
2. Follow the diagram for pattern instruction. These Cross Stitches are worked up from the lower left hole, span over 1 empty hole, and go down into the back at the 3rd diagonal hole.
3. You can work a Half Cross Stitch across the row, then reverse and do the second half or you may complete each stitch individually. Both methods are correct; however, remember to keep all stitches in the same direction.
4. When you have completed your embroidery, finish your pillow according to our pillow directions (pp. 41–42).

Notes and Options

These colors may be changed according to your personal taste.

The pillow can be finished off with tassels at the corners or twisted cord around the edges (see p. 152 and 154).

The square may also be used as a doily if you prefer. The edges should be folded under and hemmed.

Embroidered sampler

Sampler
(finished size 12 inches x 17 inches)

13-inch x 18-inch piece of Panama or Herta counted-thread fabric (7 holes to 1 inch)

Small quantities of yarns of different textures, weights, and colors

#13 tapestry needle

Sewing thread to match background fabric

1. Fold under a ½-inch hem; first on the two long sides, then across the top and bottom. Pin them in place after lining up the holes in the layers of fabric.
2. Secure the hems with a Running Stitch in doubled sewing thread.
3. Our sampler was begun with a border of red Running Stitches around the four sides. The inside border is worked in blue Cross Stitches.
4. To begin your inner pattern skip over 1 row of holes. In the next row, do 1 row of Running Stitches in green. Whip through the Running Stitches with hot pink (do not go through the back of the fabric).
5. Skip 1 row; do 2 rows of Running Stitches in green. Whip through the double rows in turquoise.
6. Skip 2 rows; do 1 row of Double Running Stitches in gold.
7. Skip 1 row; do 1 row of hot pink Running Stitches. Next alternate your Running Stitches in hot pink and then repeat the row of hot pink. Skip 1 row.
8. Do 2 rows of Half Cross Stitches leaning in opposite directions; the first leaning right, the second leaning left.
9. Skip 1 row. Do 1 row of orange Double Cross Stitches (covering 3 holes).

Leave 2 holes between Double Cross Stitch "flowers" for the rows of small gold Cross Stitches. Finish the stem and leaves with Straight Stitches going from the center of the double cross down, spanning 4 holes.

10. Skip 1 row. Do 1 row of green Backstitches.
11. Skip 1 row. Do 1 row of hot pink Cross Stitches.
12. Skip 1 row. Do 1 row of purple Straight Stitches spanning 3 holes, skipping 1 hole between each line. Do 1 row of gold Backstitches over the middle of the Straight Stitch.
13. On the next row do 1 row of red Double Cross Stitches spanning three holes leaving 1 hole between.
14. On the next row do 1 row of Running Stitches in turquoise leaving 1 hole between stitches. Do 1 row of purple Straight Stitches from the space left and down 1 space.
15. On the next row do 1 row of green Running Stitches.
16. On the next row do 1 row of yellow Half Cross Stitches slanting right spanning two holes.
17. On the next row do 1 row of orange Running Stitches. Whip through them with brown yarn.
18. On the next row do 1 row of yellow Half Cross Stitches slanting left.
19. On the next row do 1 row of green Running Stitches.
20. On the next row do 1 row of hot pink Straight Stitches covering 3 holes, skipping 1 hole between the lines. Do a Running Stitch in purple crossing over every other vertical line.
21. Skip 1 row and do 1 row of green Straight Stitches covering 2 holes.

Weave a piece of yarn through the row.

22. Skip down 4 rows to start the turquoise Blanket Stitches which will cover 3 holes. (This leaves one row of holes between the top of the Blanket Stitches and the preceding row.)

23. Skip 2 rows. Do 1 row of red Straight Stitches spanning 3 holes; leave 1 hole between each group of 3 stitches. Do Running Stitches in gold to cover the 3 stitches.

24. Skip 1 row, do 1 row of hot pink Backstitches.

25. Skip 2 rows, do 1 row of green Chain Stitch.

26. Skip 2 rows. Make the purple flowers of 3 Straight Stitches radiating from 1 center hole. The green stem and leaves are done the same way with the stem extending over 1 more hole to reach the base of the flower.

27. Skip 1 row. Do 1 row of Half Cross Stitches slanting right and then 1 row slanting left in ombré yarn.

28. Skip 1 row. Do 1 row of blue Half Cross Stitches. Cross over them with purple for a two-tone effect.

29. Skip 2 rows. Do 1 row of Double Cross Stitches in hot pink spanning 3 holes and leaving 1 hole between each flower. In the fourth row below begin 1 row of green Blanket Stitch so that every other vertical line of the Blanket Stitch becomes the stem of the flower.

30. Skip 1 row. Do 1 row of Backstitches in purple.

31. Skip 2 rows. Do gold Running Stitches in the next 2 rows. Whip through the double row with hot pink yarn.

Notes and Options

You will find stitch directions by referring to the index.

This is a good way to learn and review stitches and color combinations and end up with a lovely finished project.

This sampler can be enclosed in a glass frame or hung from a dowel.

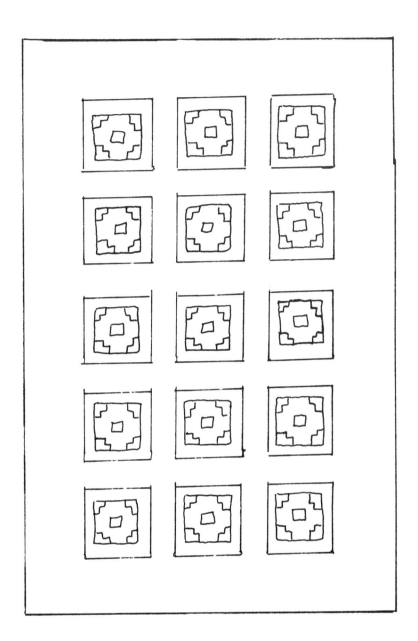

Double Cross Stitch Jute Rug
(finished size 31 inches x 21 inches)

34-inch x 24-inch piece of counted-thread jute canvas

Cotton rug yarn or acrylic, or doubled 4-ply Orlon or worsted yarn:

   3 skeins main color A (royal blue)

   1 skein color B (turquoise)

   1 skein color C (olive green)

   1 skein color D (gold)

   1 skein color E (red)

#50 doubled tan sewing thread to sew jute hems

#18 tapestry needle

Crewel needle for sewing

Thimble

Pins

Scissors

Tape measure

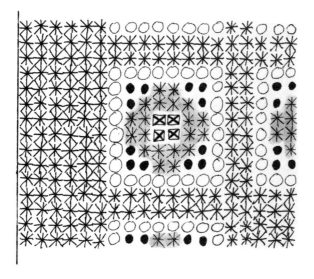

Stitch pattern

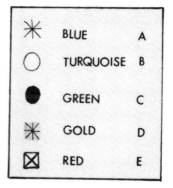

Color key

✳	BLUE	A
○	TURQUOISE	B
●	GREEN	C
✳	GOLD	D
⊠	RED	E

The jute material we have selected has dark brown threads woven through it marking off 10-hole squares which are used as guides for the pattern (see our shopping information, pp. 157–158).

1. Place the jute on a table. Leave a 3-inch unworked border on all sides which you will turn under for a hem after you have completed the stitching.
2. Start at one narrow end and, with color A (royal blue), begin the Double Cross Stitch border. Each stitch is to span over 1 unworked center hole. The left side and top of the first Double Cross Stitch will touch the woven guide lines of the canvas.
3. Work a border of 6 rows around the 4 sides.
4. With color B (turquoise), begin at the top left-hand corner inside the border and work the first pattern. It consists of 8 Double Cross Stitches to form a square.
5. With color C (green) work 3 Double

Cross Stitches inside each corner of the preceding square.
6. Follow the diagrams for the inside pattern of color D (gold). The center is 4 Cross Stitches of color E (red).
7. Repeat the pattern until completed.
8. When the stitches are finished turn the rug, right side down, and turn in the hems; first the long sides and then the short sides. Try to make the corners as neat as possible. Pin them in place.
9. Secure the hems with matching thread using a running or double running stitch.

Notes and Options

Keep a supply of needles threaded with different colors of yarn for greater efficiency.

If you wish you can add rug binding or burlap lining to the back of the rug.

Small rugs can be slippery on a wood floor. Use this rug as an attractive accent on carpeting or under a small table.

4
Appliqué

Appliqué is the technique of adding one fabric to another to achieve a decorative effect. This can be done by sewing, gluing, or using an iron-on bonding material. The fabric to be applied should have simple clear outlines and should not ravel in order to make tracing, cutting, and sewing easier.

Appliqué in itself is attractive; but it can be further embellished by the addition of embroidery. (See our embroidery section for stitch suggestions.)

Needles

Long, sharp-pointed embroidery or crewel needles with a large eye for easier threading are used for the simple Running Stitch we suggest.

Thread

In our projects we have used six-strand embroidery floss, perlé cotton, and yarn.

Fabrics

For background, you can use any firmly woven material or felt. Please note that loosely woven fabrics such as burlap do not keep their shape as well. For the appliqué, itself, felt and fabrics which fray as little as possible are most suitable.

We do not recommend turning under a hem on the appliquéd edge because this would require too much finger control for the not so nimble. Instead, we prefer the use of iron-on bonding material placed between the layers to control the raveling. Store-bought embroidered motifs, packaged individually or by the yard can be helpful too. Lace or crochet doilies can add a touch of nostalgia to a project. A printed background with solid color shapes applied makes an interesting variation.

Stretchers or Frames

Stretchers or frames will support your work. They also help in the placement, pinning, sewing, and embroidering of your design by keeping your fabric taut.

Stitching

A simple Running Stitch is used for attaching all appliqués to the background (unless you are bonding or gluing). If you are more adept, try a Blanket or Chain Stitch around the edge.

Apple Patch

8-inch x 8-inch piece of ticking
5-inch x 5-inch piece of red dotted Swiss
A few strands of dark green embroidery floss
5-inch x 5-inch piece of fusible webbing
Needle
Thread
Pins
Tape measure
Tracing paper
Transfer pencil

1. Turn under a ½-inch hem all around on ticking. Pin and stitch this hem using a Running Stitch.

2. Cut out apple from dotted Swiss, using our pattern, tracing paper, and transfer pencil.

3. Cut fusible webbing from the same transfer as the apple. Place the apple-shaped webbing directly under the dotted Swiss apple. Press the two together—to the ticking fabric—according to manufacturer's directions.

4. With 3 strands of embroidery floss

Apple patch pattern

work the apple stem in Straight Stitches and a Running Stitch to make the curved line at the top.

Notes and Options

This patch may be used as a pocket by attaching it to clothing on three sides and leaving top side open. Of course you may choose other fabrics and other designs if you wish. The patch may also be used as an appliqué for an overall, shirt, or jacket.

Nosegay Picture

15-inch x 15-inch piece of black fabric

Starched crochet doily, old or new about 9–11 inches in diameter

A piece of printed fabric with clearly defined flowers which can be cut out easily. The quantity of fabric depends upon the number of flowers you can cut out of it to cover the doily.

Piece of iron-on bonding material (buy the packaged square, not the narrow strip) sufficient to fit under each flower

Embroidery needle

Black thread

Thimble

Pins

Embroidery scissors

Ruler

1. Place the background fabric on the table. Center the doily on the fabric and pin it in place. Stitch the outer edges of the doily to the background fabric using a Running Stitch as inconspicuously as possible as you catch the doily edges.
2. From the printed fabric, select and cut out those flowers which appeal to you. Arrange them in a pleasing manner on the doily and pin in the center of each flower. (You may have to add or discard flowers for an attractive effect.) Overlapping the flowers is more artistic and working from the top of the picture downward is simpler.
3. Remove one flower at a time. Place it on top of the iron-on bonding material (Stitch Witchery or Poly Web) and cut the bonding material in the same shape as the flower. Pin both pieces back to the original position and repeat this process for all flowers.
4. Iron the flowers onto the doily following the manufacturer's instructions.
5. Put the "nosegay" into a 14-inch x 14-inch frame.

Notes and Options

This can also be a decoration for a pillow. You will then need a piece of black fabric 13 inches x 26 inches.

For an additional decorative effect, you can embroider the outline of the flowers. (See directions for making pillows pp. 41–42).

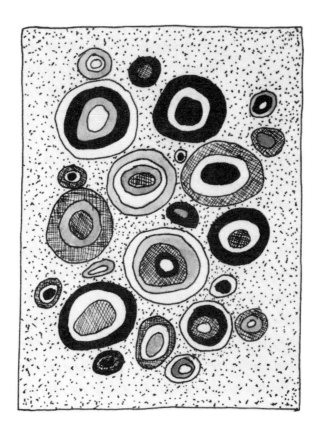

Frankly Fake Felt Flower Picture

11-inch x 14-inch piece of black felt
9-inch x 12-inch pieces of assorted colors
    of felt to cut into circles.
    1 turquoise
    1 hot pink
    1 bright yellow
    1 orange
    1 purple
Embroidery floss, 1 skein each:
    pink
    yellow
    orange
    hot pink
    purple
Embroidery needle
Thimble
Pins
Scissors
Tape measure
Varied-sized drinking glasses or other round objects from which you can trace concentric rounds of colors.

1. Cut circles of felt in varied-sized rounds so that you can make a grouping of mixed color "flowers" with 3 or 4 layers of concentric rounds. For example:
   4″ diam. hot pink, orange, or turquoise
   3″ diam. red, purple, or hot pink
   2″ diam. purple, hot pink, or orange
   1″ diam. orange, yellow, or purple

2. Make some additional felt rounds of 1-inch and 2-inch diameters for "buds." For example:

2-inch diameter	*1-inch diameter*
orange	turquoise
yellow	purple

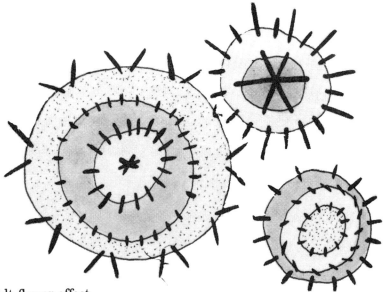

Fake felt flower effect

3. Place the flowers on the black felt background in a pleasing arrangement, putting the small buds among the larger flowers.
4. Put a few pins in each piece to hold them in place.
5. With contrasting colors of yarn do Straight Stitches radiating from each circle outward. Do one layer at a time so the stitches overlap 2 colors of felt. The stitches do not have to be even or very straight as long as they give a radiating effect.

6. This "picture" can fit in a standard size frame.

Notes and Options

This is a simple project which allows you full freedom with color. The brighter and more contrasting the felt and floss the better.

The cut-out rounds do not have to be perfect circles. A few wiggly lines and irregular circles add interest.

Round Felt Flower Pillow
(13½ inches x 13½ inches)

2 14½-inch x 14½-inch pieces of medium weight fabric for the pillow front and back.

¼ yard orange felt (If you are able to purchase small squares, you can buy five 8-inch squares of varying shades for your petals.)

¼ yard green felt or three 8-inch squares for leaves and round flower center.

Embroidery floss, 1 skein each:
orange ombré split into 3 strands
green ombré split into 3 strands

12-inch round pillow form or Dacron stuffing

Crewel needle

Thimble

Scissors

Tape measure

12-inch embroidery hoop (optional)

1. I was lucky enough to own a round tray with a 14-inch diameter to use as a pattern. Check your kitchen cabinets for a large round object to use in outlining the circle on the pillow fabric.

2. Cut the circle shapes on the 2 pieces of fabric. Put 1 aside for the pillow back.

3. Place the pillow front right side up. Locate the center by folding the fabric in half horizontally and then vertically and mark it. Put the fabric aside.

4. Trace the first petal shape onto the green felt and use it as a pattern from which to cut out 9 orange felt petals.

5. Trace our leaf shape on the green felt and use it as a pattern for 9 green felt leaves.

6. Place the petals on the pillow front so that they radiate out from the center mark. They should overlap a bit for a more natural look. Pin them in place.

7. Tuck the green felt leaves between the petals so that the petals overlap

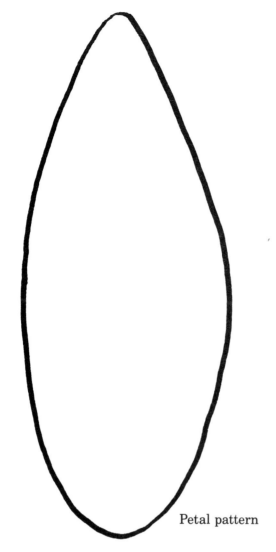

Petal pattern

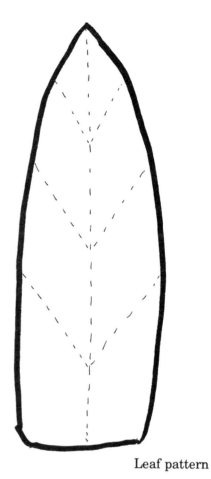

Leaf pattern

the bottom of the leaves. Pin them
in place.

8. Stitch the petals with orange floss
by doing a Running Stitch along the
edges.

9. Stitch the leaves by doing a Running Stitch along the edges and
through the center of each leaf. You
can add Straight Stitches slanting
away from the center line for a more
natural look.

10. Remove the pins.

11. Cut a circle of green felt for the
flower center. (Use a drinking glass
to trace the circle or use our pattern.)

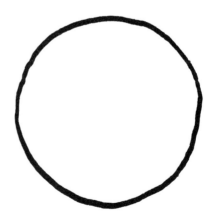

Round flower center

12. Pin the green circle in position and embroider it using green floss in a Running Stitch around its circumference and then make large straight uneven stitches radiating out from the center.

13. To finish your pillow, place the front and back fabrics, right sides together, and pin around it ¾ inch in from the edges. Leave at least a 10-inch opening in which to insert the pillow form. A 6-inch opening is adequate for pillow stuffing.

14. Using a Double Running Stitch or a Backstitch, stitch the side seams of your pillow together. Remove the pins.

15. Turn your pillow cover to the right side and stuff it.

16. As carefully as possible stitch up the opening.

Notes and Options

You may vary the shape, size, and color of the petals to suit your own taste. If your sewing stitches are not too neat, you can add fringe or twisted cord around the pillow edges (see directions pp. 151 and 154).

Blossoms in a Bowl Wall Hanging
(finished size 14 inches x 18 inches)

16-inch x 20-inch piece of natural color fabric for background

3-inch x 11-inch strip of brown felt for the table top

5-inch x 8-inch piece of gold felt for the base

6-inch x 8-inch piece of green felt for leaves (see leaf pattern)

Strips of white machine-embroidered flowers sold in trimming departments. These can be cut apart and used individually. If possible buy ½ yard of assorted sizes; if you do not have that choice, buy enough to give you a full bouquet.

16-inch wooden dowel

30-inch piece of cord for hanging

Embroidery floss, 1 skein each:
   olive green for stems and leaves
   yellow
   orange

Crewel needle

Sewing thread in natural color

Thimble

Pins

Scissors

Tape measure

1. Place the natural color fabric, right side down, and turn in a 1-inch hem on both long sides and on the narrow bottom end. Pin the hems in place.

2. With matching thread stitch the hems with a Running Stitch.

3. At the top end, turn under a ½-inch hem and turn it under again to make a casing for inserting the dowel (do not close the sides of the casing). Pin and sew using a Double Running Stitch or Backstitch.

4. Turn the piece right side up and place the brown felt 2 inches above the bottom hem. Pin and sew.

5. Cut the gold felt into a bowl shape by folding it in half; draw half the bowl so that the fold of the felt is the center of the bowl and cut out the doubled piece. The bowl will be symmetrical.

6. Cut the green felt into leaf shapes (see our leaf pattern p. 72).

7. Arrange the individual flowers on the background fabric in a pleasing manner, scattering the smaller ones among the larger ones. Pin them in place.

8. With green floss, embroider your stem with an Outline or Whipped Running Stitch (see embroidery directions p. 45) radiating from the bowl outward to the flowers.

9. Arrange the leaves emerging from the stems. Pin them in place.

10. With green floss, split into 3 strands, embroider the leaf markings with a Running Stitch.

11. With yellow and orange floss embroider over the flowers doing a Double Cross Stitch over the centers or Straight Stitches radiating from the center out to the petal tips. You need only a few stitches to enhance the flowers.

12. Insert the dowel through the casing. Knot the cord at both ends of the dowel for hanging.

Notes and Options

You can use any variety of flowers and colors for the bouquet.

The table top and bowl shapes may be embroidered on the backing instead of the felt appliqué. Doubled 4-ply yarn used in a Split Stitch gives an interesting dimensional effect.

5
Simple Weaving Through Fabric

This type of weaving is an easy technique for the not-so-nimble as it can be done even by those who have little finger dexterity. It does not require a loom or a weaving frame. You can weave through mesh curtain fabrics, even-weave fabrics such as Panama cloth or monk's cloth. The only tools needed are a thimble, a large tapestry needle, a tape measure and a scissors. A long-shafted, large-eyed weaving needle can also be used for easier handling.

All weights and textures of yarn can be used as long as they slide through the mesh without distorting the threads. If they do, you need thinner yarn.

The patterns can be formed with a simple over-and-under stitch through the mesh. All rows can be done as you worked the first row, or you can alternate the stitches of each row. For instance:

Row 1—over-under-over-under

Row 2—under-over-under-over

The pattern and the color arrangement are your creative choice.

Weave-Through Shawl

18 inches x 72 inches (2 yards) of scrim
    (an evenly woven mesh curtain fabric)
3 1-ounce skeins of 4-ply Orlon:
    color A (blue)
    color B (pink)
    color C (yellow)
Large tapestry needle or a weaving nee-
    dle with a large eye and a long shaft
Package of small hairpins (these hold
    better in mesh than straight pins)
Scissors
Tape measure

Fabric

For our background we used an inexpensive white rayon scrim 18 inches x
72 inches with 2 spaces to an inch in the
length and 3 spaces to an inch in the
width. Any similar fabric can be used as
well.

Yarn

We selected 4-ply Orlon in three colors:
blue, pink, and yellow. You can substitute any type of yarn which slides easily
through the mesh: wool worsted, rayon,
or cotton rug yarn. If your fabric is more
closely woven (more holes to the inch)
you may have to use less bulky yarn.

Hems

Lay your fabric out on the table.
Matching your meshes, turn under a
1-inch hem in the widths (the narrow
ends). Hold them in place with the hairpins. Thread your tapestry needle with a
22-inch length of yarn and weave in and
out of each space along the hems. For
these bottom hems, secure the yarn at
the beginning and end by going over the
first and last stitches a few times.

Turn under a 1-inch hem on the long sides. Hold them in place with the hairpins.

Count the number of rows in the width of your mesh. This will tell you how many strips of yarn you will need. Each strip will be 88 inches long—72 inches for the weaving through and 8 inches left at each end to form the fringe. Cut your yarn strips after you have done your color plan; we used random stripes (different widths of different colors starting with a wide border of color A). You may also do alternating colors—one stripe of each color if you prefer it.

The first row of weaving is through the hem. Do not secure your yarn; leave an 8-inch tail instead. Weave in and out of each space until you have completed the row. Repeat this procedure on the opposite long hem removing the hairpins as you work along. Continue in each long row of the mesh, working first on one side of the scrim, and then on the

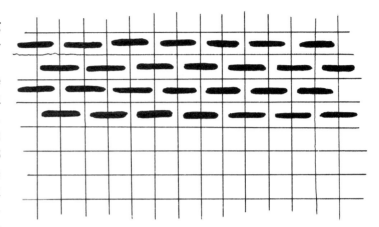

Pattern for weaving shawl

other (if you want a matched pattern) until your scrim is filled. Trim your fringe if necessary.

Notes and Options

It is advisable to wrap your cut strips of yarn around a shirt cardboard to prevent tangling.

You or your Helping Hand may knot the fringes as close to the hem edge as possible to hold them more securely.

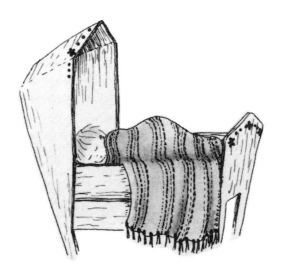

Baby Coverlet

1½ yards 36-inch white Orlon mesh with the texture of wool knit

4 1-ounce packages of assorted pastel color yarns

5 yards ¾-inch iron-on bonding (Stitch Witchery)

Large-eyed tapestry needle
Thimble
Pins or hairpins
Scissors
Tape measure

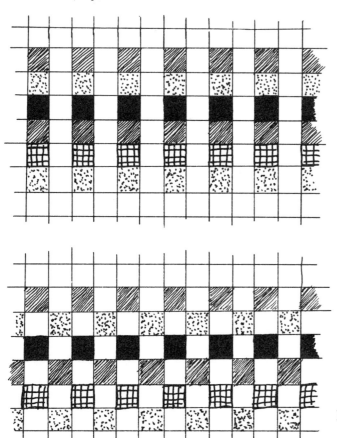

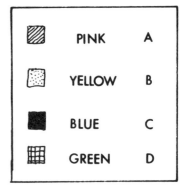

Color key

▨	PINK	A
▦	YELLOW	B
■	BLUE	C
▦	GREEN	D

Pattern for weaving coverlet

1. Cut the yarn into 36-inch lengths. Decide on your color arrangement. In our piece we used 7 stripes, each stripe consisting of 7 rows with unworked spaces between the stripes. Each stripe is made up of 1 line of each color, for example:

    color A (pink)
    color B (yellow)
    color C (blue)
    color A (pink)
    color D (green)
    color B (yellow)
    color A (pink)

    When all the stripes are completed, trim off any excess yarn at the edges.

2. Lay the fabric flat on the table, turn back a 1-inch hem on the short ends, and place the pins on the crease line. Cut 2 pieces of iron-on bonding 34 inches each. Tuck the strips under the hems and press, following manufacturer's directions. (If you are able, you can sew the hems instead.) Cut 2 pieces of the iron-on bonding material 50 inches each and repeat the procedure for the long sides.

3. You can conceal any errors by covering the hemmed edges, on the wrong side, with colored iron-on hem binding. If you wish you may add fringe on the short ends.

6 Quilting

In this chapter you will learn to do simplified quilting using fabrics of special prints, batting, backing, and a Running Stitch.

Fabrics

Select medium weight, washable fabrics which have clearly defined patterns such as patchwork prints, plaids, ginghams, or a large figure or animal design whose outlines can be used as guides for stitching. Dacron batting is available in a rolled sheet package and sold in needlework shops and some variety stores. Batting is not the same as pillow stuffing so be sure that you purchase the correct product.

The backing fabric should be the same or slightly lighter in weight than the print so that the needle can penetrate the three layers easily. In our projects the quilt backing is visible in the finished piece; however, the tote bag has

the addition of a lining, the pillow has the addition of stuffing and a pillow back.

Needles and Thread

We suggest that you use a long, sharp-pointed embroidery needle and strong polyester or cotton thread (#50 or #60) for the stitching. A thimble is absolutely essential.

Technique

1. Place the backing on the table wrong side up.
2. Cut the Dacron batting (doubled for quilts, single for the bag and pillow) and place it to fit over the backing.
3. Your printed fabric goes on top, right side up.
4. Pin the three layers together working from the center out to the edges. To keep your quilting evenly puffed,

80

smooth the top fabric outward as you pin. You can follow either the outline of your print or pin in a geometric fashion (following selected lines of ginghams or plaids) until the three layers are well anchored. Be generous with your pinning.

Sewing

5. Beginning at the center, baste outward with large stitches where you have pinned. Remove the pins.
6. Do a Running Stitch appropriate for your fabric. If you are using a patchwork pattern, follow the outlines of the printed patches; if you are using a block print follow the outlines of the blocks; if you are using a large animal print follow the lines of the animal.
7. Remove your basting stitches.

Finishing

Each project has specific directions for finishing, which can be embellished with embroidery stitches on the outlines for an old-fashioned handmade look. Ready-made embroidered motifs may be placed in strategic positions.

Patchwork Tote Bag

18-inch x 36-inch piece of patchwork print fabric

18-inch x 36-inch piece coordinated color fabric for lining

Piece of quilt batting 17 inches x 35 inches

1 pair of bag handles (ours are 2 dowels with knob ends)

2 30-inch strips of twisted cord for handle straps

Embroidery floss split into 3 strands. Select a few colors to contrast with the print.

Sewing thread to match the lining fabric

Crewel needle

Thimble

Pins
Scissors
Tape measure
Hoop (optional)

1. Place the patchwork print fabric, right side down. Center the sheet of batting over it. Next, arrange the lining fabric, right side up, over the batting.
2. Pin the three layers together starting at the center and radiating from that point. (Follow the general quilting directions pp. 80–81.)
3. Baste where you have pinned. Remove the pins.
4. With embroidery floss of a contrasting color, embroider along the outlines of the printed patches. Use a Chain Stitch, Blanket Stitch, Cross Stitch, or Whipped Running Stitch to achieve an authentic look. (See our embroidery section for stitch directions, pp. 44–46.)
5. When your embroidery is completed, turn under the edges of the printed fabric and turn under the edges of the lining fabric ½ inch. Push in any batting protruding be-

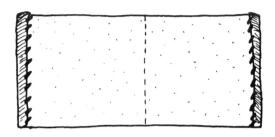

Stitching pattern

tween them, so that your seams will be easier to sew. Pin the edges together on all four sides.
6. With matching thread, do a Running Backstitch or Overcasting Stitch to secure the sides.
7. With your print fabric facing down, fold over a 2-inch casing at each narrow end in which to insert the bag handles.
8. Pin across and stitch the casing with an Overcasting Stitch.
9. Insert the bag handles through the casing and screw on the end knobs.
10. Knot "straps" just inside the knob ends of the handles.

Notes and Options

This bag may also be worked on striped or plaid fabric.

Baby Quilt

(finished size 34 inches x 46 inches, ruffled edging not included)

Piece of print fabric 36 inches x 48 inches

Doubled batting to measure 34 inches x 46 inches

Piece of woven coordinating gingham 36 inches x 48 inches

5 yards of ruffled eyelet edging

Needles

Thread

Thimble

Pins

Scissors

Tape measure

1. Place the print fabric right side down on a table. Place the batting directly over this, then the third layer. This is the backing which, in a quilt, becomes the underside.

2. Pin the centers and the corners together and turn the complete piece over, print side up.

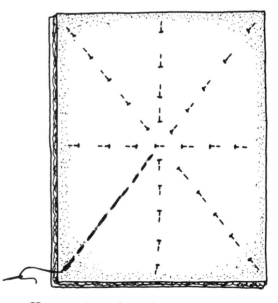

How to pin and stitch

3. Begin pinning the pieces from the center to the outer edges to keep the puffing even (see pp. 80–81).

4. Baste the three layers together where you have pinned. Remove the pins. (Don't be concerned about absolutely straight lines here as these stitches are temporary.)

5. Find the vertical and horizontal centers of the quilt by folding the piece in half in each direction. Pin generously along the center vertical line using the gingham boxes as an easy guide. From the center line, measure 4 inches on either side for the next vertical row. Repeat the procedure until all vertical stitching 4 inches apart is completed.

6. From the horizontal center mark, repeat the above procedure. (Keep smoothing out the top fabric as in general quilting directions.)

7. To finish the sides of the quilt, turn under a 1-inch hem on all four sides of the front and back fabrics. The hems should face in toward one another. Ironing them is helpful.

8. Push in any excess batting at the edge so that you will not have to sew through its thickness.

9. Insert the heading of the ruffling between the folded-in hems of the front and back fabrics, pinning all three layers together (be generous with pins).

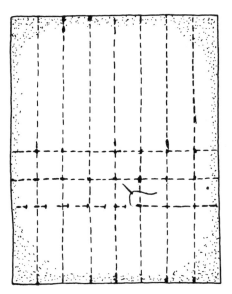

Proper vertical and horizontal lines

10. Stitch the three layers with a Double Running or Backstitch using matching thread.

11. Fold under the cut ends of the ruffled trim where they meet and stitch them together.

Notes and Options

Colored embroidery floss split into 3 strands may be used instead of matching thread to achieve a more decorative finish.

If you do not want a ruffled edge you can simply stitch the front and back layers together. A 2-inch-wide bias binding in contrasting color may be added.

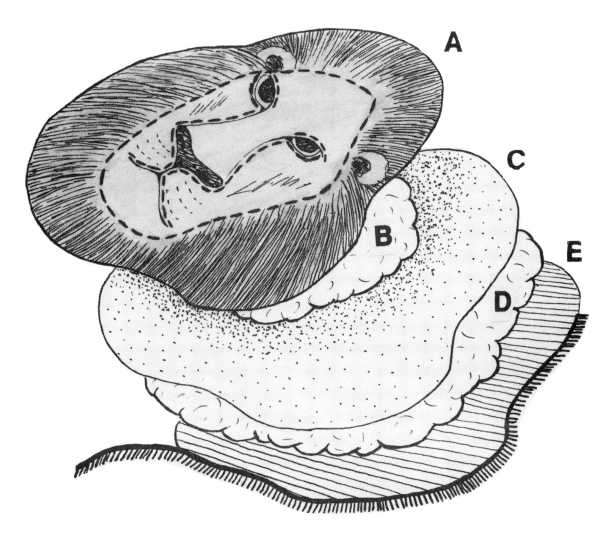

Lion's Head Pillow

1 lion's head 12 inches x 14 inches cut out of an animal print fabric(A). We selected an animal print with a large lion's head. The shape of the pillow back is the same as the large print motif selected and cut out. Use the print motif as the pattern for the back shape. You can use any clearly defined motif 10 inches x 10 inches or larger, such as a flower, animal, or human face (see shopping information, pp. 157–158) and obtain an equally good result following these directions.

1 piece solid color fabric cut to the size and shape of the cut-out print motif for the pillow back (E)

1 piece of batting or stuffing for quilting fill of the same size as the fabric (D)

1 piece of thin cotton fabric to line the batting of the same size (C)

Dacron stuffing to fill the pillow (B)

Fringe (optional); we used it around the edges of the lion's head to give the effect of a lion's mane

1 skein of embroidery floss to outline the features (we used brown)

Sewing thread for seams

Crewel needle

Thimble

Pins

Scissors

Tape measure

1. Cut out ½-inch seam allowance around the shape of the lion's head following the outline of the print fabric.

2. Place the lion's head print right side down. Place the batting over the print and the thin lining over the batting right side out. Additional pieces of batting can be inserted for more fullness in the lion's cheeks and eyes. Pin the three layers together. Turn them right side up.

3. With your embroidery floss, working from the center out, do a Whipped Running Stitch or Backstitch on the lines around the areas which are to be quilted for emphasis. We stitched around the face, the eyes, the nose, and the mouth to give the lion an outstanding head.

4. Remove the pins and place your quilted piece, face down with the pillow back fabric over it right side up to make the pillow case. (See our pillow instructions for stuffing and finishing pp. 41–42).

5. For the lion's head we added gold and brown fringe around the outside seam; for a large flower green fringe would be attractive.

Notes and Options

There are also many fabrics suitable for children which lend themselves to this type of outline quilting.

This is an easy project, using only a few lines of creative stitchery to give an amusing three dimensional result.

7
Needlepoint

Needlepoint is simply stitchery on evenly woven canvas mesh. Traditionally, it differs from embroidery in that the needlepoint stitches cover the canvas completely. If you can sew or embroider, you can also do needlepoint, using larger needles, heavier yarn, and a larger-gauge canvas such as gros point, quick point, rug, or plastic. The number of threads per inch determines the gauge of the canvas. We urge you to avoid those finer than #10 (10 threads per inch) and even this count should only be used for stitches which cover more than two spaces.

There are two types of canvas:

1. *Mono canvas* is made of single threads intersecting. It is preferable to try this type first as it is a bit easier on the eyes. All stitches except Half Cross Stitch work well on it.
2. *Penelope canvas* is made of double horizontal threads intersecting double vertical threads. In our projects we count the double threads as single. After you have used penelope canvas, you will find that it holds its shape better than mono canvas in addition to giving you a fuller-looking stitch. It may be used for all stitches; however if you wish to use it for Bargello patterns be sure that your yarn is thick enough to cover the double threads.
3. One of our favorite background materials for the not-so-nimble is a pliable, white mono plastic mesh. This is not expensive and can be purchased in many needlework departments and through catalogues. It is manufactured in various sizes and shapes. The smaller circles and squares can be used for coasters, key ring tags, or appliqués. The largest size sheets are 10½ inches x 13½ inches. We use these for tote bags, book covers, eyeglass cases, and pic-

ture frames. The holes are evenly spaced, 7 to 1 inch, making them clearly visible. The mesh cannot be pulled out of shape so it needs no blocking. In most cases, no frame is needed; however, if you do need a frame, secure the top of the plastic sheet to the top of the stretcher frame with long tacks. Leave the bottom unattached so that you can reach under for your needle. You must be careful not to split the meshes as they cannot be mended; therefore you must never force too large a needle through the holes. Aside from these cautions, we strongly recommend this product for easy working of all projects requiring a stiff backing. It is not, however, soft enough for pillows.

Needles

Blunt size #18 tapestry needles—easy to thread—are suitable for most projects. For a 3–5 hole canvas, you will find that #13 needles have an even thicker shaft and larger eye.

Yarn

Because of the gauge of the canvas we use, the usual Persian and tapestry yarns are too fine and too expensive. Instead we suggest 4-ply worsted, 4-ply Orlon (doubled in some cases), 6-ply synthetic, cotton, or wool rug yarn. Whatever you choose should easily slide through the mesh spaces while at the same time adequately covering the background. Keep your working yarn length no more than 18 to 20 inches to avoid tangles and arm fatigue. Having a few threaded needles ready will be time saving. Remember to buy sufficient yarn of matching dye lots.

Frames

Needlepoint frames of many styles or an inexpensive stretcher frame can hold your work firmly and help prevent distortion of the canvas. An easily rotated frame is the best because most stitches require turning the canvas for each row. For those who work with one hand, it is essential; for others it is optional. You have to determine which method is more efficient for you, so try both. If you purchase a stretcher frame, it should be secured to a table with 2 C-clamps (available at the hardware store). Attach the C-clamps over the top of the frame and under the edge of the table so that your project extends beyond the table, allowing you to work freely. Embroidery hoops are not suitable for needlepoint.

Design

The designs should always be clearly defined and simple. Intricate shapes and small details cause confusion and should be avoided. You will achieve successful results with geometric patterns, contemporary designs, interesting color schemes, and a few simple stitches.

Start and Finish

For all but plastic canvas, mark off an additional 2 inches around all sides. This unworked allowance will be helpful in attaching your canvas to a backing, since it is easier to sew through. If your canvas has a *selvage* (a tape-like edge), it should be the side of your piece. To prevent raveling, all cut edges must be either folded back and basted with a Running Stitch or taped with masking tape folded neatly over the edges. It is advisable to identify the top of your canvas by placing a mark on it (either a pen mark or Cross Stitch will do).

When starting your needlepoint, push the threaded needle up from the underside leaving a 3- or 4-inch tail of yarn below. Catch this tail under your first few stitches to hold it and cut off any excess yarn.

To finish off (when you have 3–4 inches of yarn left on your needle) push the needle to the underside of the canvas, turn the canvas over, and weave through 4 or 5 completed stitches. Don't forget to cut off the excess yarn as these tails of yarn will cause tangling.

Technique

Needlepoint is properly done in 2 steps: If you are right-handed, use your right hand to insert the needle into the face of the canvas; use the left hand under the canvas to catch the needle and return it through the canvas to the front of the piece. If you are left-handed, reverse the order: left hand on top, right hand below. This two-handed motion may seem clumsy at first; but after practicing you will soon develop a rhythm and find it less tiring. If you must use one hand, it will have to do both motions. Here are a few valuable bits of information:

1. Never pull your stitches too tightly.
2. If your yarn becomes tightly twisted while working, simply allow your threaded needle to drop freely and it will unwind itself.
3. When putting your project aside, roll rather than fold it.
4. To remove errors, cut the affected stitches carefully with a pointed embroidery scissors and remove the threads with a pair of tweezers.

5. Attach your finished work to a backing with wrong sides together, whenever possible. It is simpler and neater than turning its thickness inside out.
6. If you are left-handed, you can turn the graph directions upside down for working.
7. Blocking your work will require the assistance of a Helping Hand since it must be pulled straight and taut and tacked to a board (which we feel is too difficult for the not-so-nimble).
8. If it is too difficult for you to turn the canvas at the end of each row, you may end your yarn at the end of the row. Begin the next row at the side where you originally began. Follow this procedure throughout.

Stitches

We suggest a few basic stitches which will be easy for you to learn and use. These stitches are of two types: straight and slanted.

1. The straight *Gobelin* is the simplest, fastest to work, and quickest to cover the canvas, as it goes up and down covering two or more meshes at a time. It can be done from either direction. The pattern is created by the arrangement of the stitches either in a horizontal line or stepped up and down to give a flame-like effect. You need no printed canvas, but only the ability to do elementary counting. Once you or your Helping Hand have plotted your first row, the succeeding rows follow in order.
2. The easiest slanted stitch is the Half Cross Stitch which is worked left to right (for the right-handed) on

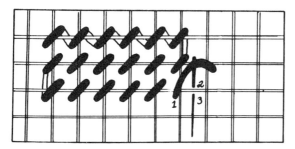

Half Cross Stitch

Continental Stitch

penelope canvas. Your stitches will always slant toward the right. At the end of your first row, turn your canvas around (so the top is at the bottom) and work as you did the first row—from left to right.

3. Cross Stitch can be worked on both types of canvas. On penelope (double thread) canvas, work a row of Half Cross Stitches (going from left to right). When you reach the end of a row or section begin working in the reverse direction (right to left) crossing over the Half Cross previously

made, to complete your Cross Stitch. When working on mono canvas, complete both diagonals of the first stitch before continuing on to your second Cross Stitch. It gives a better appearance if all the top diagonals are worked in the same direction.

4. Continental Stitch can be used on both types of canvas working from right to left. Your stitches will always slant toward the right. Continental Stitches use more yarn; but they give more fullness making your project wear better.

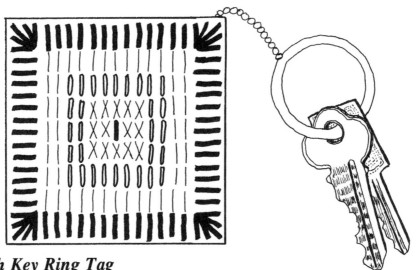

Plastic Mesh Key Ring Tag
3-inch x 3-inch plastic mesh square
(19 holes x 19 holes)

3-inch x 3-inch piece of felt in coordinating color

Small amounts of doubled 4-ply Orlon or worsted or cotton or acrylic rug yarn.

#18 tapestry needle
Crewel needle
Sewing thread
Thimble
Scissors
Ruler or tape measure
Key chain (as pictured in the diagram)

This is a simple project to make with leftover pieces of plastic mesh or small squares packaged four to a bag.

1. The stitch used is a simple Straight Stitch (upright Gobelin) spanning 1 empty hole (see the stitch direction p. 89). The pattern is a square in a square of mixed colors. The side stitches of the outside border are worked horizontally. All the other stitches are vertical.
2. When your stitching is completed, insert the chain into a corner hole.
3. Center the felt lining over the back of your canvas. Pin to the back of the worked stitches. Sew the piece around the edges with an Overcasting Stitch catching the back of your needlepoint stitches.

Notes and Options

Any variation of stitches, color, and design may be used to cover the mesh for this practical, easy-to-make project.

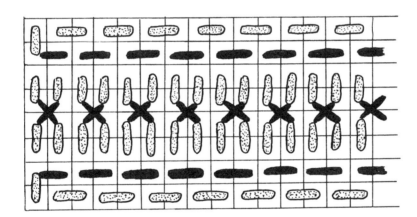

Embroidered Belt on Rug Canvas

4-inch width of rug canvas (4 holes to 1 inch). (The length is determined by the waist measurement plus 4 inches.)
Strip of 2-inch-wide ribbon or bias binding the same length as the canvas for lining.
Cotton, acrylic, or wool rug yarn:
    color A 7 yards (blue)
    color B 5 yards (red)
or any color combination you wish.
Sewing thread to match lining
#13 tapestry needle
Crewel needle for sewing lining
Thimble
Pins
Scissors
Tape measure
Belt buckle (optional)

1. Place the strip of canvas on your table and bend in 1-inch along the top and bottom lengths. Carefully match up the holes in the folded layers of the canvas. You should have 8 rows of holes to embroider. Embroider together hems on narrow edges, using a Running Stitch in color A (blue), going into one hole and coming out the next.

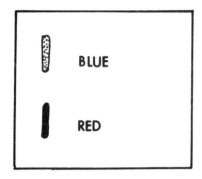

Color key

2. With the right side facing you, on row 1, begin your embroidering with color A (blue) and do a Running Stitch across the length of the belt going into one hole and coming out in the next hole of the mesh.

3. On row 2, using color B (red), do a second row of Running Stitches; but alternate the position of the stitches from the previous row so that you have a woven effect.

4. On the next 2 rows, work an Upright Gobelin (a vertical straight stitch) in color A (blue).

5. Turn the belt upside down and repeat the 3 rows of stitches you have done at the top.

6. With color B (red), do 1 row of Cross Stitches in the middle of the belt connecting the ends of your blue Gobelin Stitches.

7. Turn the belt to the wrong side for lining. Place the ribbon along the length of the canvas. Turn the edges of both the ribbon and the canvas under and toward each other inside the belt and pin in place.

8. With matching thread and a Running Stitch attach the lining to the wrong side of the belt.

Notes and Options

The belt can be secured with a buckle, a button and loop, large-sized hooks and eyes, or dots or strips of Velcro or Scotchmate flexible fabric fasteners.

This is a quick and easy project which can be varied in width, color, and stitchery for all age groups.

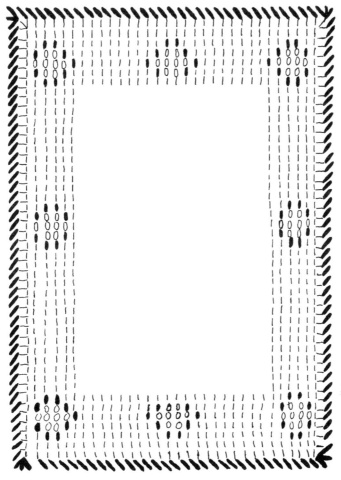

Picture Frame

1 sheet 10½ inches x 13½ inches of plastic mesh can make 2 frames 5 inches x 7⅛ inches with an open area for a snapshot 3 inches x 5 inches.

1 piece of felt 5 inches x 7 inches in a matching color for the lining.

Doubled 4-ply Orlon or worsted yarn, acrylic or cotton rug yarn which can go through the holes easily:

1 ounce main color A (pale green or medium blue)

5 yards color B (dark green or navy blue)

2 yards color C (hot pink or red)

Sewing thread to match felt lining

#18 tapestry needle

Thimble
Pins
Scissors
Ruler or tape measure

Color key

1. Cut the plastic sheet to measure 5 inches x 7⅛ inches (these directions are for one frame).

2. Begin your work with color A. This design is done in a vertical Straight Stitch worked from the left-hand corner down into the space directly below and continuing across the row. Follow the diagram for the design. The dark lines are dark green; the thin lines are pale green; the circles are hot pink.

3. When you have completed the pattern, finish off the sides with color B, worked in an Overcasting Stitch.

4. Place your felt lining over the back of the canvas and pin it in place.

5. With matching thread and small Running Stitches secure the lining.

6. A 3-inch x 5-inch picture can be glued to the mesh.

7. A loop of yarn can be sewn to the top of the lining for hanging, or you may insert this frame into a commercial glass frame of the same size.

Notes and Options

Now that you have the idea, you can make your frames in all sizes and shapes and in various patterns.

If you do not enclose the frame in glass, use a protective fabric spray to keep it clean.

Eyeglass case

Eyeglass Case (Large Size)

1 sheet 10½ inches x 13½ inches plastic
   mesh
2 pieces of felt 3½ inches x 7 inches for
   the lining in a related color
Doubled 4-ply Orlon or worsted yarn,
   acrylic or cotton rug yarn, which can
   go through the holes easily, 1 ounce
   each:
   main color A (black or blue)
      color B (gold or red)
      color C (brown or white)
Sewing thread to match felt pieces
#18 tapestry needle
Thimble
Pins
Scissors
Ruler or tape measure

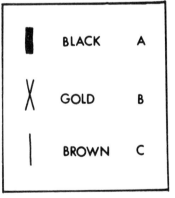

Color key

1. Cut the plastic mesh to obtain 2
   pieces, one for the front and one for
   the back of the case, each to measure
   3½ inches x 7 inches (or 24 x 27
   holes).

2. Take one piece of plastic mesh and

begin your work with color A. This design is done in Gobelin Stitch (a simple vertical stitch), which will be worked from the first hole to the third hole below it, skipping over the middle hole. The only pattern change is in the center medallion where you will work from the first vertical hole to the hole directly below it without skipping over the space.

3. I have worked my initial into the center medallion. But, instead of an initial, you can continue with the single stitches if you like. If you want to use another initial, plan it out on graph paper first.

4. When the pattern is completed on both pieces of plastic mesh, place the pieces of felt lining on the wrong side of the mesh and pin them in place.

5. With sewing thread and a Running Stitch, stitch the linings around the edges.

6. Place the two lined pieces, wrong sides together. Using your main color yarn, join with an Overcasting Stitch around the two long sides and one narrow side (bottom of case).

7. The fourth side remains open for inserting the eyeglasses. An Overcasting Stitch is used around the top edge of each side, though, to finish them off.

Notes and Options

The dimensions of the case may be changed for different sizes of glasses. If you want your case narrower, eliminate the stitches from the sides; your center pattern will remain the same.
Medium Case
3 inches x 7 inches
Narrow Case for Half Frames
2½ inches x 7 inches
Use a protective fabric spray to keep the case clean.

Rainbow-Striped Pillow
(finished size 10 inches x 10 inches)

1 piece mono needlepoint canvas (7 holes to 1 inch) 12 inches x 12 inches

1 piece coordinated color fabric for pillow backing 12 inches x 12 inches

Dacron stuffing

Cotton, acrylic, or wool rug yarn or doubled 4-ply Orlon or knitting worsted, 1 ounce each:

color A (royal blue)

color B (turquoise)

color C (purple)

color D (red)

color E (hot pink)

color F (orange)

color G (bright yellow)

color H (white)

Sewing thread to match pillow back

#13 tapestry needle

Crewel needle for sewing

Thimble

Pins

Scissors

Tape measure

Frame (optional)

above it and push the needle down into the hole above them. Bring the needle back up in the space directly to the right of the first stitch insertion. Continue completely across the first row for the straight border.

5. For the second stripe, repeat as above with the same color for the first 30 stitches, skip the next 10 spaces and continue with 30 stitches to the end of the row.

6. For the third stripe, start as you did the second stripe by working 30 Straight Stitches with your color B. Fill in the ten blanks in the second stripe with the color of stripe 3 (B). Finish your row as before.

7. Repeat all rows in the same manner with different colors. This "jump" in the center is an easy way to get an

Stitch pattern

1. Bind the edges of the canvas with masking tape.

2. An upright Straight Stitch (Gobelin) spanning 2 empty meshes is the simple stitch used for this pillow.

3. Measure in 1 inch from the top and 1 inch from the left side of the canvas. Repeat this on all four sides and mark it with a marking pen for the unworked border.

4. Begin your first stitch at the left side. Insert your needle with color A into the 4th hole below the top border line. Skip over the 2 empty holes directly

intricate looking design.

8. When you have completed your stitching, finish your pillow according to our pillow directions (pp. 41–42).

Notes and Options

You can use any mixture of coordinating colors or two or three alternating stripes of different shades of one color with effective results.

This pillow can be trimmed with tassels at the corners or twisted cord around the edges. (See directions for tassels, p. 152 or twisted cord, p. 154.)

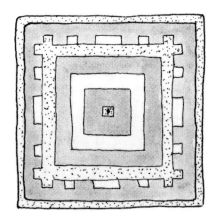

Half Cross Stitch Geometric Pillow

16-inch x 16-inch piece of #5 penelope canvas (5 holes to 1 inch)

16-inch x 16-inch of fabric for pillow backing

Dacron stuffing or 14-inch x 14-inch pillow form

Rayon, cotton, or Orlon rug or bulky yarn, doubled 4-ply Orlon, or worsted yarn thick enough to cover the canvas adequately. We used:

45 yards color A (bright red)

65 yards color B (bright blue)

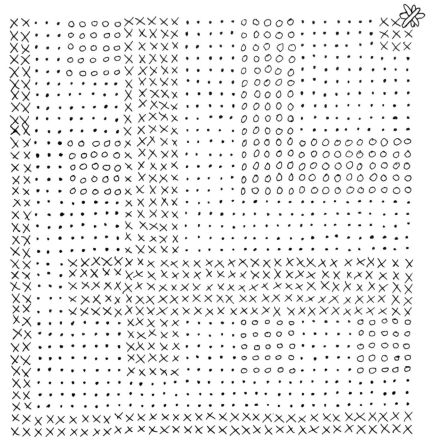

Stitch pattern

25 yards color C (gold)
#18 tapestry needle
1-inch-wide masking tape
Thimble
Scissors
Tape measure
Needlepoint frame (see frame information)

1. Fold the masking tape over the raw edges of the canvas to prevent raveling. Draw an X to identify the top of the canvas. This will ensure the direction of your Half Cross Stitch, which must always slant from the lower left to the upper right.
2. Locate the center of the canvas: Fold the canvas in half vertically and mark it, then fold it in half horizontally and mark it again.
3. With color C, do a Double Cross Stitch at the center. Your pattern will work outward from this area.
4. Follow the diagram to see that the pattern works out evenly from the center. There are 2 rows of color A all around the center cross, then 7 rows of color B, 5 rows of color C, 5 rows of color B, 5 rows of color A.
5. The variation at the inner motif is worked in squares of 5 stitches.
6. The outside border consists of 3 straight rows of color B and two rows of color A.
7. When you have finished the pattern follow our general directions for making a pillow (pp. 41–42).

Notes and Options

Your Helping Hand can copy this pattern onto the canvas with an indelible marking pen which can further simplify the project for you.

It will be more efficient if you keep a supply of needles threaded with different colored yarns ready to work.

You can add a twisted cord trim or tassels at each corner made of matching yarn; see pp. 152 and 154.

This pattern is dramatic enough to be used as a contemporary picture.

Square in square Continental Stitch pillow (general effect)

Square in Square Continental Stitch Pillow
(finished size 13 inches x 13 inches)

14-inch x 14-inch piece penelope rug
  canvas (4 holes to 1 inch)
14-inch x 14-inch piece of brown fabric
  for pillow backing
Dacron stuffing or 13-inch square pillow
  form
Cotton, acrylic, or wool rug yarn, thick
  enough to cover the mesh adequately:
  32 yards color A (brown)
  14 yards color B (terra cotta)
  16 yards color C (light gold)
  7 yards color D (turquoise)
  12 yards color E (olive green)
  13 yards color F (deep gold)
Sewing thread to match backing
#13 tapestry needle
Crewel needle for sewing
Thimble
Pins
Scissors
Tape measure
Frame (optional)

1. Bind the edges of the canvas with
   masking tape.

2. Fold the canvas in half vertically and
   mark the center; fold it in half horizontally and mark it again. This
   center is where you will work your
   first 4-stitch square of Continental
   Stitches in terra cotta yarn.

3. Remember that all the stitches must
   slant from the lower left to the upper
   right on the front of the canvas.

4. Do 2 rows of light gold Continental
   Stitches around the first (center)
   square; next is 1 row of deep gold, 1
   row of green, 1 row of turquoise, 2
   brown, 1 pale gold, 1 deep gold, 1
   green, 1 terra cotta, 1 green, 1 deep
   gold, 2 pale gold, 1 deep gold, 1 green,
   1 turquoise, 1 terra cotta, 1 pale gold,
   1 terra cotta. The border is made up
   of 5 rows of brown on all 4 sides of the
   pillow.

5. Finish your pillow by following our
   pillow directions (pp. 41–42). Needlepoint pillows are sewn together
   with the right sides out as they are
   too bulky to turn inside out.

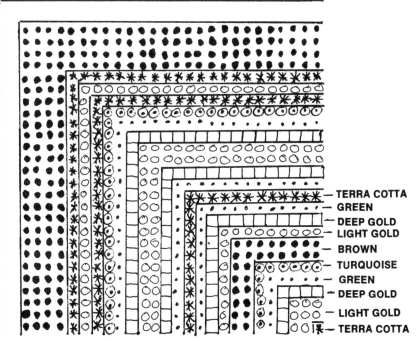

— TERRA COTTA
— GREEN
— DEEP GOLD
— LIGHT GOLD
— BROWN
— TURQUOISE
— GREEN
— DEEP GOLD
— LIGHT GOLD
— TERRA COTTA

Stitch pattern

Notes and Options

You can vary the look of these squares by changing the colors and widths.

The pillow can be trimmed with twisted cord (p. 154) around the sides or tassels at the corners. (See our directions, p. 152.)

This pillow may be worked in Half Cross Stitches, if desired.

TURQUOISE RUBY RED	PURPLE YELLOW	ORANGE GREEN
YELLOW ORANGE	BLUE GREEN	TURQUOISE PURPLE
GREEN PURPLE	RUBY RED YELLOW	BLUE ORANGE

Color key

Contemporary Patch Picture

10½-inch x 13-inch sheet of plastic mesh
Tapestry needle
Thimble
Scissors
Colored tapestry yarns (used double throughout) as follows:
    45 yards color A (emerald green)
    45 yards color B (deep purple)
    30 yards color C (ruby red)
    45 yards color D (sunny yellow)
    30 yards color E (royal blue)
    45 yards color F (deep orange)
    30 yards color G (medium turquoise)
    15 yards color H (black)

1. Following chart, begin at the top of the canvas, 1 row down and 1 row in from right. Use Continental Stitch with yarn doubled.
2. The first patch starts with 23 stitches of color G (turquoise). The outer border of all the square-in-squares is made up of 3 rows of stitches. The first inner square is color C (red). (The second patch is directly next to the first.)

3. The second patch border is color B (purple). The inner circle is color D (yellow). Follow the pattern to form the shapes. You will note that it is impossible to make a perfect circle in needlepoint since it is worked on squares; therefore, only an impression of a circle is possible.
4. The third patch border is color F (orange); the inner square is color A (green).
5. Work the second row of patches directly below the first. In the second row, the first patch border is color D (yellow), the inner circle is color F (orange).
6. The center patch border is color E (blue), the inner square is color A (green).
7. The third patch in the second row has a border of color G (turquoise) and an inner circle of color B (purple).
8. In the third row of patches, the first patch has a border of color A (green) and an inner square of color B (purple).

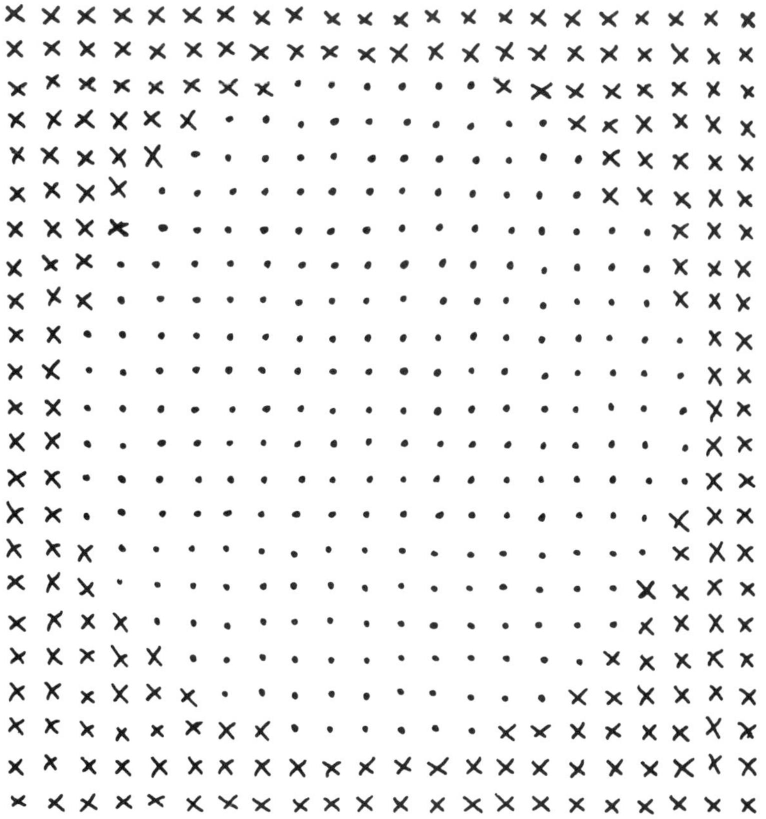

Circle pattern

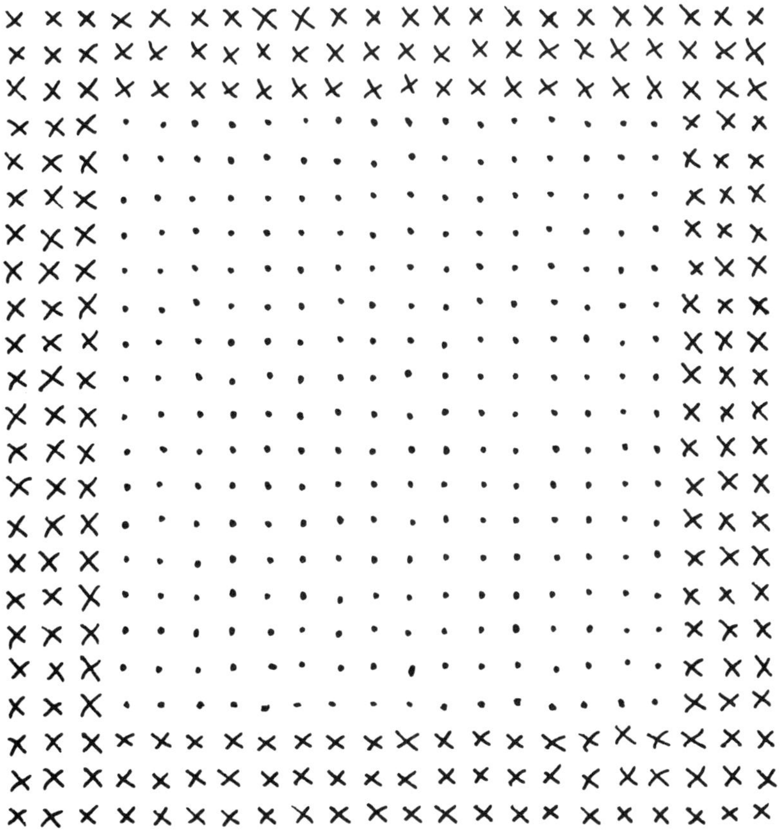

Square pattern

9. The second square has a border of color C (red) and an inner circle of color D (yellow).
10. The last patch has a border of color E (blue) and an inner square of color F (orange).
11. When all patches are completed, work 1 row of black stitches around all four sides.
12. Carefully trim off excess mesh.
13. Finished size should measure 10½ inches x 10 inches

14. This picture can be attached to a piece of stained plywood, 2 inches larger all around, or it can be placed in a commercial frame.

Notes and Options

You may change the choice of colors to suit your taste. You may substitute doubled Orlon or worsted yarn.

Small Bargello Rug
(finished size 19 inches x 24 inches)

23-inch x 28-inch piece of rug canvas (4 holes to 1 inch)
Wool, cotton, or acrylic yarn thick enough to cover the meshes adequately.
31 yards color A (olive green)
49 yards color B (bright gold)

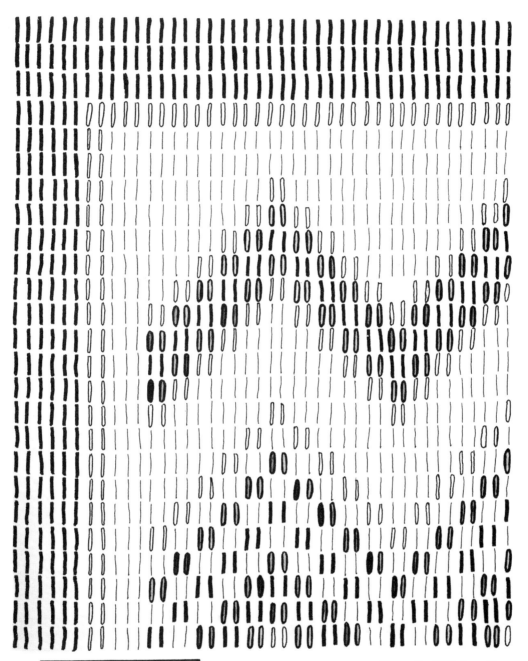

Bargello Stitch pattern

▮	GREEN	A
◖	GOLD	B
│	WHITE	C
◗	RUST	D

Color key

25 yards color C (white)
20 yards color D (rust)
#13 tapestry needle
Thimble
Large pins or large hairpins
Scissors
Tape measure or ruler

1. Fold back the canvas for 2-inch hems, first on the long sides, then on the narrow sides, lining up the holes in both layers. Pin the hems in place. (Hairpins hold the mesh well.)

2. Turn the canvas right side up and begin the stitching in the first hole at the top left corner with color A (olive green). Your stitches will go through the two layers of canvas (the top and the hem). The border begins with a row of Straight (Gobelin) Stitches. *Each stitch spans 3 holes of the canvas* for the entire rug except the last row of Overcasting at the edges of the rug. Each row consists of 84 stitches across.

3. The border begins with 3 horizontal rows across the narrow ends of the rug. The side (vertical) borders are 6 stitches wide—all in color A (green).

4. With color B (gold) work 1 row across the narrow ends; and 2 rows of gold worked vertically down the 2 sides.

5. With color C (white) work 2 rows across and 3 rows down.

6. With color C (white) work 1 row across for 10 stitches, skip 2 spaces (left for the top of your Bargello pattern) and continue for 18 stitches; skip 2 spaces; continue for 18 stitches, skip 2 spaces and finish your last 10 stitches.

7. On the next row with color C (white) work 8 stitches, skip 6, work 14, skip 6; work 14; skip 6 and finish with 8 stitches.

8. On the next row with color C (white), work 6 stitches across; go to the row below and work 4 stitches across; go to the row below and work 2 stitches across.

9. On the row below change to color B (gold), do 2 stitches to begin the 6 double steps up of your Bargello pattern. Follow the diagram and count the stitches of the first Bargello row carefully. Your Helping Hand might do one row to simplify any problem you may have. Once you have established the first row of steps, you follow in sequence, going down 5 double steps, then up again across whole row.

10. Continue following the diagram until your pattern is completed.

11. For a neater edge, do an Overcasting stitch around the outside row of the rug.

Notes and Options

Of course, you may change the colors to suit your personal taste.

You can also change the sequence of stitches by working your design out on graph paper.

Lining the rug is optional.

Bargello Tote Bag

(finished size 10½ inches x 13½ inches x 3 inches)

This was the most successful needlework project in the continued therapy program. It may take longer to complete but the results are well worth the effort. The only slight problem you may encounter is in the cutting of the canvas for the pattern. Follow the directions slowly, and one at a time. It will be simple if your Helping Hand prepares the canvas and works the first row of stepped Straight Stitches (Bargello).

3 10½-inch x 13½-inch sheets of plastic mesh (70 x 90 holes)

½ yard of felt fabric in a coordinated color for the bag lining.

1 pair of bag handles (to fit inside the 13½-inch width).

Bulky acrylic or wool or doubled 4-ply Orlon or doubled worsted, or straw yarn which fits through the holes easily but covers the plastic mesh. (Double the yardage for 4-ply worsted or Orlon.)

    100 yards color A (navy blue)
    65 yards color B (red)
    50 yards color C (natural)

Sewing thread to match the lining
#18 tapestry needle
Crewel needle (for sewing lining)
Thimble
Pins
Scissors
Tape measure or ruler
Stretcher frame (optional). Attach your
  work at the top only.

bottom of the bag. Put it aside. Strips C1 and C2 are the sides of the bag and have to be cut shorter to match the height of the back and front of the bag. Count the holes and cut across row 20 of the mesh. You will now have 22 x 70 holes of mesh on strips C1 and C2.

2. You now have 5 pieces of plastic

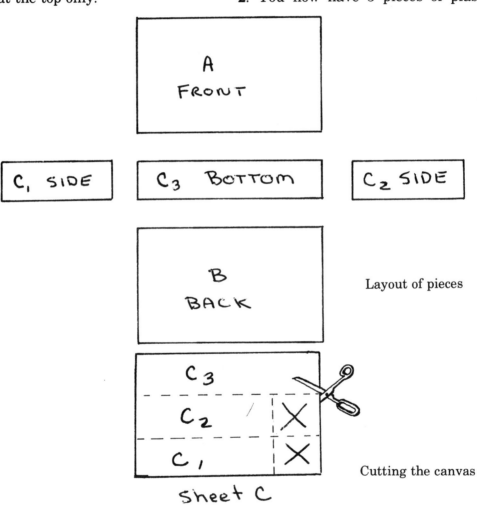

Layout of pieces

Cutting the canvas

1. The three plastic sheets are used as follows: sheet A, bag front; sheet B, bag back; sheet C, cut into three strips for the sides and bottom of the bag. This sheet is cut along the length into three equal strips of 22 x 90 holes of mesh. Cut off any excess plastic mesh neatly. Strip C3 is the

mesh. You can use these pieces as patterns for the lining by setting them on the felt fabric and tracing around them with a pen or pencil.

3. Cut out the 5 felt lining pieces, Put them aside.

4. The stitch used throughout is the Gobelin or Straight Stitch which

covers 4 holes of the canvas for all the border bands and the Bargello pattern. The only variation is in the different size Straight Stitches used to fill in the small areas between the border and the first row of Bargello

and the center medallions on sheets A and B.

The patterns for the front (sheet A) and the back (sheet B) are worked exactly the same.

The borders on all 5 mesh pieces

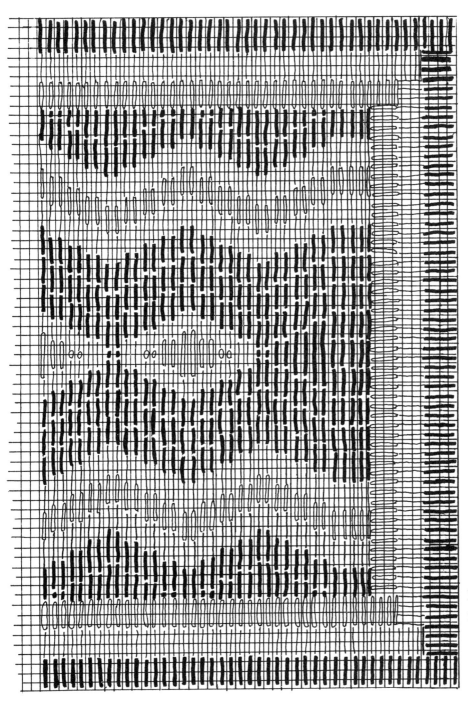

Half pattern
for front and back

consist of bands of color going around all four sides.

5. On sheet A work your 3 border bands starting at the outside with color A (navy blue). Continue with the middle band in color B (red) and the inside band of color C (natural).

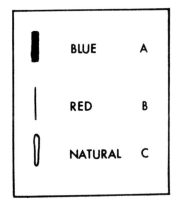

BLUE   A

RED   B

NATURAL   C

Color key

6. Start band 4 with 5 Straight Stitches (color A) in a row. Stitches 6 and 7 will start 1 mesh down (the beginning of your Bargello pattern) and end 1 mesh row below the preceding 5 stitches. Stitches 8 and 9 start 1 mesh down from the preceding 2 stitches again. Stitches 10 and 11 start 1 mesh down from the preceding pair. Stitches 12 and 13 start 1 mesh down from the preceding pair. Stitches 14 and 15 are worked *up* 1 mesh from the preceding pair; stitches 16 and 17 are worked up 1 mesh; stitches 18 and 19 are worked up 1 mesh; stitches 20 and 21 are worked up 1 mesh. Stitches 22 and 23 begin the steps down of the design. Repeat the steps up and down according to the pattern. Once you have established your first Bargello row, the succeeding rows are no problem. You merely follow the original row of steps.

7. Bargello row 2 is worked in color B.

8. Bargello row 3 is worked in color C. Bargello row 4 is worked in Color B. Bargello rows 5, 6, and 7 are worked in color A.

9. Turn the mesh sheet to work the bottom half of the mesh exactly the same as the top half. (It is preferable to work each half before working on the center medallions which are formed where the points of the Bargello pattern meet.)

10. You will find 2 empty meshes separating the areas where the Bargello points meet. Close these gaps with a short straight stitch in color A.

11. Fill in the unworked areas on the center left side and center right side of the mesh with Straight Stitches of the size required to cover the empty spaces in color A.

12. There are now 3 center medallions to be filled in. With color B follow the steps of the Bargello pattern from the preceding rows; but this time make your pairs of stitches span only 3 holes of the mesh except for the end pair of stitches on each medallion which span 4 holes of mesh.

13. Fill in the center of each medallion with Straight Stitches in color C.

14. Fill in the spaces left between the inside border band and the first Bargello row with Straight Stitches of proper size to cover the meshes.

15. Repeat these directions for sheet B.

16. For the bottom of the bag, take sheet C3 and work your 3 bands of color as in sheet A. Fill in the empty meshes in the center with color A.

17. For the sides of the bag, take sheets C1 and C2 and work the same as the bag bottom.

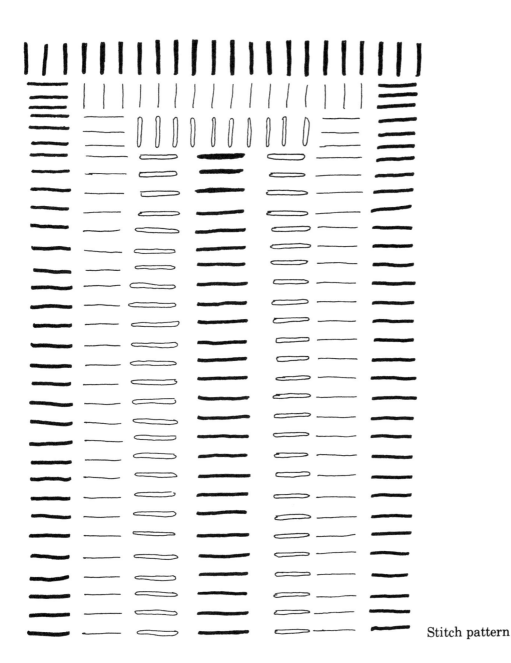

Stitch pattern

18. Pin the felt lining pieces to the wrong sides of the finished mesh pieces. Do an Overcasting Stitch (page 24) with the needle and matching thread catching the felt and plastic edges.

19. With the mesh pieces right sides together and the holes of the mesh lined up, join the sections of the bag to one another using a tapestry needle with color A yarn to work an Overcasting Stitch.

20. After all seams are sewn, do an Overcasting Stitch around the top edge of the bag in main color yarn.

21. The type of handle you use will determine the method of attaching it. Some types may have to be inserted between the lining and the mesh and overstitched to secure them.

Notes and Options

You can use a printed fabric for the lining, which requires the making of an inner bag.

Twisted cord or braid can be used as handles and attached at either side.

You may change colors to suit your individual taste.

If you are able, you can vary the design. Work it out on graph paper, with the same number of squares as there are holes in the mesh. You can work squares, stripes, or variations of Bargello.

8
Novelty Stitches

Rya or Turkey Work Loop Stitch

For our purpose, this looped stitch is done on rug canvas. Leave a 2-inch border of unworked canvas around the pattern for finishing off. Start at the bottom of the canvas and work across the row from left to right. The second row is worked above the first. Continue in this manner. A threaded #13 tapestry needle is inserted into the second hole from the left edge. Leave a 1½-inch tail on the bottom of the canvas. Turn the needle pointing to the left and come up in the first hole. Push the working yarn above the row with your left index finger and go into the third hole with your needle again turned to the left and come out in the second hole (where the tail is hanging out). Pull the knot taut. For the next stitch, hold down a 2½-inch length loop of yarn, with your left thumb. Repeat the movements of the first stitch. Your first and last stitches will be single

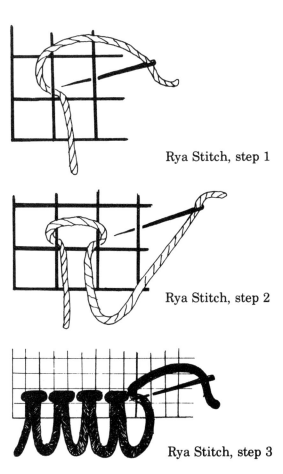

Rya Stitch, step 1

Rya Stitch, step 2

Rya Stitch, step 3

113

"fringes"; the stitches in between are loops which may be left as loops or cut to form a pile. They should be cut at the completion of each row.

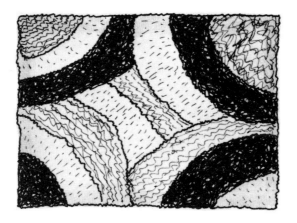

Splash of Color Rya Pillow

16-inch x 18-inch piece of rug canvas (4 holes to 1 inch). Finished size will be 12 inches x 14 inches.

16-inch x 18-inch piece of coordinated fabric for back

Dacron stuffing

Cotton, acrylic, or wool rug yarn or doubled 4-ply Orlon or worsted in varied bright colors, approximately 20 yards of each color:
color A (bright orange)
color B (bright yellow)
color C (hot pink)
color D (turquoise green)
color E (terra cotta)
color F (purple)
color G (royal blue)
color H (gold)

#18 tapestry needle
Thimble
Pins
Scissors
Tape measure
Stretcher frame (optional)

1. Bind the edges of the canvas with masking tape.
2. Measure in 2 inches from all sides for a border of unworked canvas. It will be helpful to mark off the lines of the border with a marking pen.
3. (Begin the rya stitches on the lower left of the canvas. Remember that rya is worked from the bottom row up and from the left to right side of the canvas.) Practice the stitch in the instructions (p. 113) first. The pattern is only a suggestion. It does not have to be copied exactly. It is more important to have masses of color; and this is an excellent way to use up yarn left over from other projects. Rug yarn mixed with doubled 4-ply yarn gives an interesting range of texture.
4. Copy the general idea of our design onto your canvas with a waterproof marker and fill in the areas with the suggested color scheme or your own selection. You may find stripes or

blocks of color simpler for your first attempt.

5. When the stitchery is completed, place the pillow right side down and the backing fabric centered over it (wrong sides together). On three sides of the pillow, turn in the unworked edges of the canvas and any excess fabric or backing neatly. Pin and stretch them together using a Backstitch or Overcasting Stitch. On the fourth side, which will be the opening for the pillow, turn under 2 inches at each end. Pin and stitch as above.

6. Insert the Dacron stuffing, filling the pillow adequately. Pin and finish stitching the opening, which was left for the stuffing.

Notes and Options

The challenge of this pillow is the color coordination; you can be the artist.

The rya stitch can be worked in stripes, squares, or irregular blocks of color with good results.

The seams of the pillow can be covered with twisted cord if the stitches are too visible.

Shaggy Sunflower Pillow
(finished size 14 inches in diameter)

16-inch x 16-inch piece of rug canvas (4 holes to 1 inch)

14-inch diameter Dacron-stuffed pillow form (a foam form is more difficult to finish off in this bulky pillow).

15-inch diameter circle of coordinated color fabric for the pillow back (check your kitchen cabinets for a tray or large round pan to trace).

1¼ yards of olive green fringe

Cotton, acrylic, or wool rug yarn:

30 yards color A (rust red)
35 yards color B (orange)
95 yards color C (gold)
38 yards color D (olive green)
Green sewing thread (doubled) to sew fringe and backing
#13 tapestry needle
Crewel needle for sewing
Thimble
Pins
Scissors

Tape measure
Stretcher frame (optional)

This pillow uses the rya stitch on rug canvas.

1. Bind the edges of the canvas with masking tape and mark the top.
2. Fold the canvas in half vertically to locate the bottom center. The rya stitch is worked from the bottom row up.

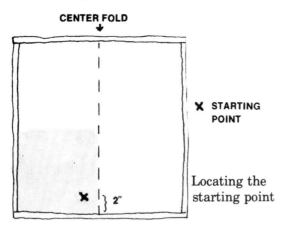

Locating the starting point

3. Leave a 2-inch border of unworked canvas and begin your first stitch 4 holes to the left of the vertical center fold. Do 8 rya stitches. The loops should measure 1–1¼ inches long. Cut off the yarn.
4. Continue, following the diagram. (You can trace the one-quarter view on a piece of graph paper and complete the circle if you find it simpler to follow.) The second row begins four spaces left and one row above the first row.
5. The diagram of concentric circles of color is given as a general guide. In this project you will not disturb the pattern if you do a stitch or two out of place. The idea is to get irregular rounds of color.
6. When you have completed the stitching, turn the worked canvas, right side down, place over it the

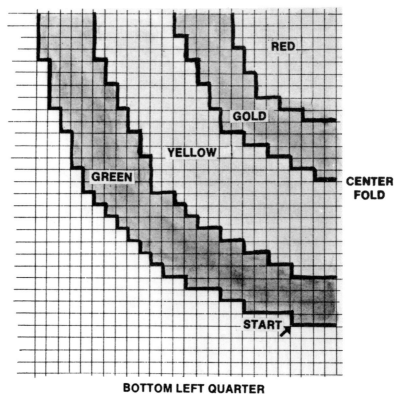

BOTTOM LEFT QUARTER

Stitch pattern

same shape you have used to trace the backing. With a marking pen, trace a circle.

7. Cut the square canvas into a circle 15 inches in diameter.

8. With the canvas, right side down, center the pillow form over it and then the lining, right side up.

9. Turn under the edge of the un-worked canvas and the edge of the lining fabric, and pin them together around the pillow form.

10. With doubled sewing thread, stitch the three pieces together using an Overcasting Stitch or Backstitch.

11. Place and pin the fringe around the pillow edge so that the heading covers the outside seam and the fringe

ends become the outer layer of the sunflower.

12. Secure the edging to the pillow edge with a Running Stitch in green thread.

13. Cut the rya loops if you wish.

Notes and Options

Leaving some of the loops uncut gives an interesting effect.

The colors of the flower may be changed to suit your personal taste.

This pillow can also be worked as a square by not cutting the canvas or backing into a circle and filling in the blank canvas with additional olive green loops.

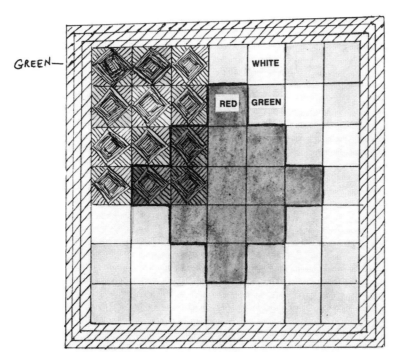

Raised Cross Stitch Rose Pillow
(finished size 13 inches x 13 inches)

Each "rose" motif is worked by following the numbers on the chart.

17-inch x 17-inch piece of #4 rug monotype canvas (4 holes to 1 inch)

15-inch x 15-inch piece of fabric for pillow back

13-inch x 13-inch square pillow form or Dacron stuffing

Acrylic, cotton, or wool rug yarn or doubled 4-ply Orlon or wool (Cut all yarn into 45-inch lengths for each rose.)

    98 yards green

    39 yards white

    43 yards rose red

Matching sewing thread

#13 tapestry needle

Thimble

Scissors

Ruler

Stretcher or needlepoint frame (optional)

Masking tape

1. Bind the edges of the canvas with masking tape to prevent raveling.
2. Measure 4½ inches down from the top edge and 2¾ inches in from the left side to start the #1 stitch of the first rose pattern.
3. This raised stitch is worked on an 8-square base, beginning with a diagonal Cross Stitch covering 8 holes of the canvas. Following the numbers on the chart is an amusing game with an attractive result. Remember to bring the needle up to the front of the canvas for odd numbers on the chart and down to the back of the canvas for even numbers. Work the stitches by following the numbers in order 1, 2, 3, 4, etc.

3 U	8 D	16 D	24 D	25 U	17 U	9 U	2 D
11 U							6 D
19 U							14 D
27 U							22 D
26 D							23 U
18 D							15 U
10 D							7 U
1 U	5 U	13 U	21 U	28 D	20 D	12 D	4 D

8-square pattern for 1 motif.

On horizontal rows the #1 stitch of the second rose will be in the same hole as #4 of the first rose. When starting the second horizontal row, remember that the bottom holes of the mesh of the first rose are also the top of the roses in the second row; they share the same hole so there is no unworked mesh between them.

When you have completed all 7 horizontal roses and all 7 vertical roses you can begin the border consisting of 3 rows of Continental Stitch around the square of the pattern.

Complete the pillow according to our pillow directions (pp. 41–42).

Notes and Options

This pattern may be done on all sizes of canvas and, while it may be done in 10- and 12-stitch squares, the 8-stitch square is the simplest.

You may further embellish your pillow by using twisted cord, binding or tassels. (See pp. 152 and 154.)

9
Crochet

Crocheting is a craft requiring dexterity in both hands; however, I've found it less difficult than knitting. If you are able to handle the working materials it can be a most pleasant occupation.

If at one time you did fine crocheting but now find it difficult to handle, all you have to do is enlarge your viewpoint. Use a larger hook, heavier yarn, bolder color, and simpler patterns.

Learning by watching and practicing the actual stitches is the best way to master the art of crocheting. You will understand the technique better, if you find a Helping Hand to show you how. It will save a lot of wear and tear on your nerves if you observe hook, yarn, and finger motions. You can then review by checking with the diagrams presented in this chapter.

Hooks

Hooks H, J, and K are used for our projects and your ease.

Yarns

Four-ply knitting worsted, 4-ply Orlon, or 4-ply acrylic of the same weight work best with these hooks. You may also use bulky yarns with a K hook.

Colors

The color selection is vast and includes solids as well as ombrés (shades of the same color), variegated (multicolored), and tweeds. Generally, multicolor yarns are fun to work with and can even cover up an occasional error.

Joining New Yarn

It is preferable to join a new ball of yarn at the end of a row. But in certain instances you may come to the end of the yarn in the middle of the row so don't panic. Knot the ends together (leaving 2-inch tails). When the project is completed, weave in the loose ends with either a needle or a hook.

Sewing Seams

To sew a seam in crochet, pin your pieces, right sides together, and with a blunt-end tapestry needle and the same yarn, overcast edges with medium tension (see directions p. 24).

Blocking

If you are a perfectionist, you may block your work by gently passing a warm iron over a damp cloth placed flat on your project. Blocking is optional for our purpose.

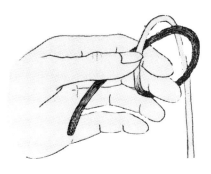

Forming a slip knot, step 1

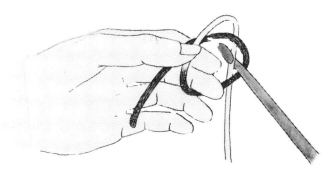

Forming a slip knot, step 2

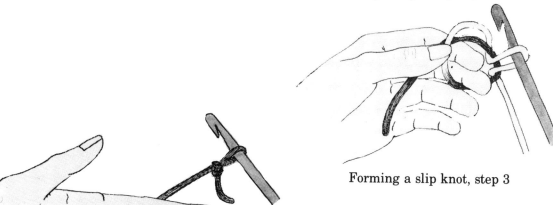

Forming a slip knot, step 3

Hand position at start of chain, step 1

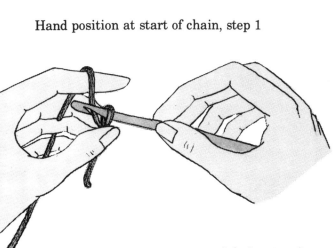

Hand position at start of chain, step 2

Crochet Basics

Making a Chain

To make a starting chain for crochet, form a slip knot on the crochet hook which is held in your right hand (if you are right-handed). With the loop on the hook, place the hook (pointing to the left) under the strand of yarn from the skein and draw it through the loop already on the hook. Repeat this procedure until you have the required number of stitches.

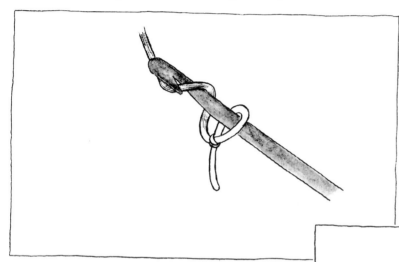

Making a chain, step 1

Making a chain, step 2

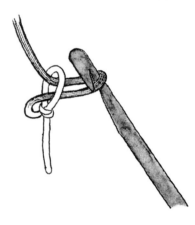

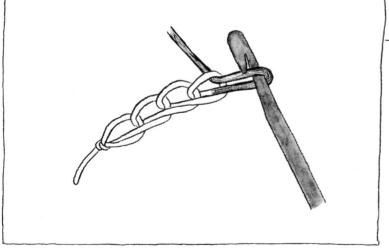

Making a chain, step 3

Single Crochet

Put the crochet hook through the two top loops of the second stitch from the hook. Catch the strand of yarn from the skein and pull it through the loops.

Catch the yarn from the skein with the hook once more and pull it through the remaining two loops on the hook. Repeat this procedure for the required number of stitches.

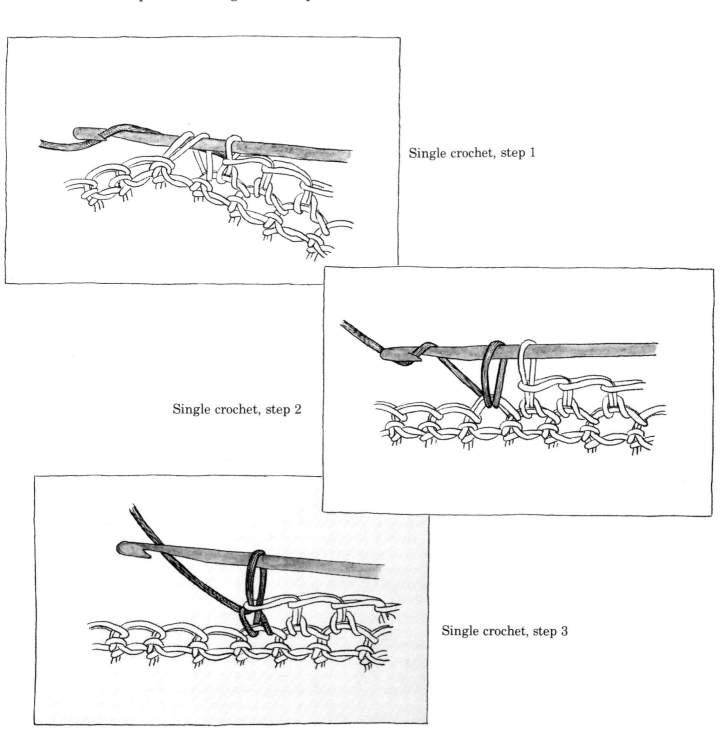

Single crochet, step 1

Single crochet, step 2

Single crochet, step 3

Double Crochet

Catch the strand of yarn from the skein with the hook, wrapping it around the hook and put the hook with the loop on it through the stitch in the row below it. Catch another loop from the yarn on the skein onto the hook and pull it through the same stitch below. (You should now have three loops on the hook.) Catch the yarn from the skein and pull it through two of the three loops. Catch the yarn from the skein and pull it through the remaining two loops. Repeat this procedure for the required number of stitches.

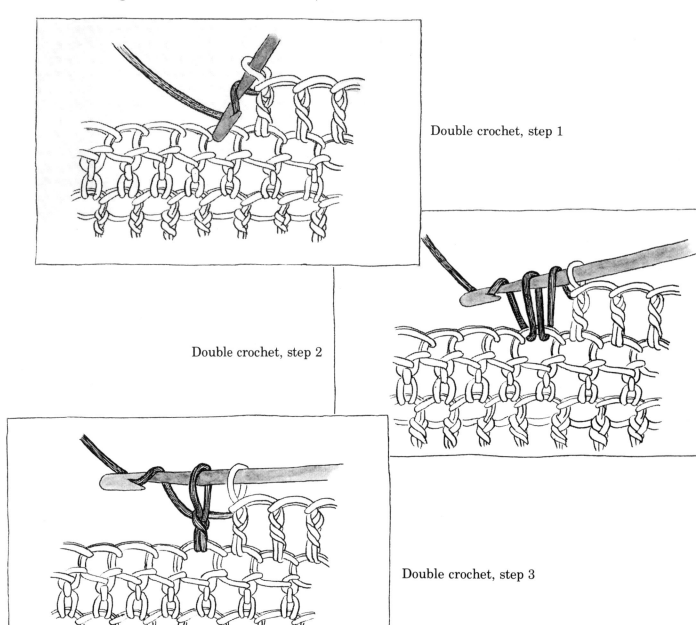

Double crochet, step 1

Double crochet, step 2

Double crochet, step 3

Scarf worked lengthwise

Long Scarf
(finished size 60 inches x 6 inches)

6 ounces knitted worsted or Orlon or acrylic

Size K crochet hook

1. Make a chain approximately 60 inches long.
2. Row 1, chain 2, single crochet in 3rd stitch from hook (this allows for the turn). Single crochet in each single crochet across. Chain 2, turn.
3. Row 2, single crochet in back loop only of each single crochet across. Chain 2, turn.
4. Repeat Row 2 until desired width is reached.
5. Cut yarn and weave in ends.

Notes and Options

By the way, it is not vital to follow the number of stitches exactly. It can be varied to suit you. The width can also be adjusted.

This scarf also works out attractively in ombré yarn. (Don't forget ombré yarn usually comes in a 3½-ounce pack.)

The ends may be finished in two ways:
1. Thread a needle with the yarn and do a Running Stitch across the end width. Pull tight and secure by going over the last stitch three or four times. You may attach a matching or contrasting wool tassel by sewing it to the gathered edge.
2. Attach a fringe to the ends of the scarf (see page 151).

Child's Red Crochet Hat

2 4-ounce balls big bulky wool (Orlon does not have the give or elasticity of wool.)
Size K crochet hook

You are making a rectangle which you will sew together lengthwise.

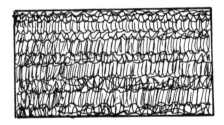

1. Chain 38. (Should measure 15½ inches in length.)
2. Row 1, double crochet in 4th chain, from hook, double crochet in each chain across (36 double crochets, counting chain 3 as 1 double crochet). Chain 3, turn.
3. Row 2, skip first double crochet, double crochet in back loop of each double crochet across. Double crochet in top of chain 3; 36 double crochets.
4. Repeat row 2, 18 times more. Cut yarn and weave in ends.
5. Thread a tapestry needle with matching yarn.
6. Overcast long sides together to form a tube. Run a strand of yarn through

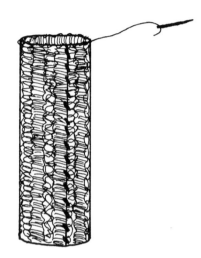

every other stitch at the top end of the tube, draw tightly together and fasten securely.
7. Turn up lower edge to form cuff.

Notes and Options

You may add a pompom to the top, if you wish (see p. 153).

Sleeveless Vest

(size 12)*

3 3½-ounce skeins of ombré knitting
  worsted or Orlon or Acrilan
Size H crochet hook

1. Start at side edge and chain 152 stitches.
2. Row 1 (right side), single crochet in 3rd chain from hook and 1 single crochet in each chain across (150 single crochets). Chain 1, turn.
3. Row 2, work in *back* loop only of each single crochet in 1st row, single crochet across, chain 1, turn. Continue to work in back loop only. Repeat row 2 until there are 28 rows.
4. Make a second rectangle the same as the first.
5. Place the rectangles side by side, wrong sides up. Overcast (see p. 24) the edges of the pieces together with matching yarn in a yarn needle for 58 stitches (center front). Cut yarn and weave in end. In the same manner, overcast from the other ends of rec-

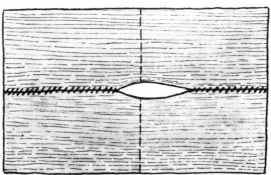

Flat view with front and back seams sewn

tangles, placed side by side, for 47 stitches (center back). Cut yarn and weave in end. Fold rectangles in half, right sides together. You can now see the shape of the vest.
6. Sew side seams with Overcasting Stitch (see sewing instructions) from the bottom up for 9 inches to the armhole.

Notes and Options

Of course this vest can be made in a solid color.

*For size 14, add 6 inches to starting chain and add 4 more rows to each rectangle (2 more ridges).

Introduction to Granny Squares

The granny square is a magical pattern which lends itself to endless projects and yet is easy to do and handle. A hook, some yarn, and a small scissors are tools which are readily portable. What a wonderful way to play with colors and incidentally use up odd amounts of yarn!

To make a traditional granny square, you need learn only a chain stitch, slip stitch, and double crochet. And after you've made your first square, there'll be no holding you back; the world is yours. You can make a pot holder or a rug, depending upon your yarn, your hook size, and of course, your ambition.

Directions for Granny Square

dc = double crochet
3 dc = 1 shell
ch = chain stitch
st = stitch
means repeat directions within

1. Place slip knot on crochet hook and

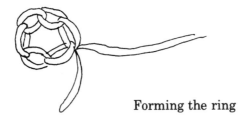

Forming the ring

chain 6. Join first and last ch with slip stitch to make ring.
2. Ch 3, work 2 dc in middle of ring just formed *, ch 1, 3 dc in ring *. Repeat directions within last * three more times, then ch 1, end round with slip stitch to top st of original ch 3. Cut

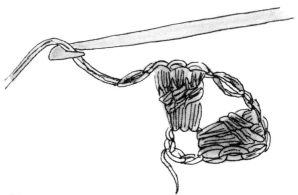

First corner showing two shells

yarn, leaving a 2-inch end for weaving in. Tie on new color in center of any corner (ch 1 space).
3. Ch 3, make 2 dc in same space, this equals one "shell"; ch 1, make 3 dc in same space (this forms a corner). Ch 1. In following ch 1 space make 3 dc, ch 1 and another 3 dc (again a corner is made). Make 2 more corners. You

Working the second round

have now formed a small square motif. Cut yarn, leaving a 2-inch end. Tie on new color for round 3 in center of any corner (ch 1 corner space).
4. Ch 3, 2 dc, ch 1, 3 dc in same space (another corner is made) * ch 1, 3 dc in next ch 1 space (not a corner), ch 1 and work two shells with ch 1 between in next corner.* Repeat till square is complete. Cut yarn, leaving

128

end. Tie on new color in any ch 1 corner space.

5. Ch 3, 2 dc, ch 1, 3 dc (first corner). Ch 1, shell (3 dc) in next ch 1 space. Ch 1, shell (3 dc) in next ch 1 space. Ch 1,

Finished square

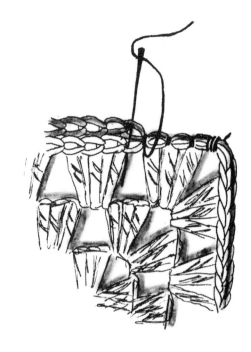

Two squares joined by overcasting

shell (3 dc) in ch 1 of corner, ch 1, shell (3 dc) (second corner). Continue around until square is complete and you have reached starting corner. Join with slip stitch to top of ch 3. Break yarn.

6. To join squares, first pin them, then thread a yarn needle with main color. Place squares right sides together. Starting at a corner, making sure that shells of each square match each other, overcast, catching top stitch of both squares.

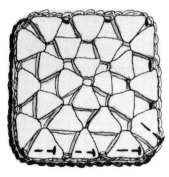

Two squares pinned for sewing together

Notes and Options

Squares can be made of solid colors.

Squares can be made of different colors. This is more effective if outside row is always the same color. Some examples of color combinations you might try are:

round 1	shocking pink	or	gold
round 2	turquoise	or	orange
round 3	emerald green	or	rust
round 4	royal blue	or	dark green

Working with black yarn causes eye strain. Using ombré yarn can be very effective. It is multicolored and does away with choosing colors for each row (it also camouflages any errors). To further enhance your squares, made with ombré yarn, a row of single crochet in a contrasting color is most dramatic. This row is made by doing a single crochet in each stitch and 3 single crochets in each corner stitch.

Granny Square Hat

2 ounces 4-ply knitting worsted
Size J crochet hook

1. Each square will be approximately 5 inches. Make 5 squares.
2. With right sides together, pin 4 squares side by side, so they form a wide band.
3. With a tapestry needle and yarn that matches the last row of each square, do an Overcasting Stitch (see p. 24).
4. Place the fifth square on top of the sewn band.
5. Pin together on all 4 sides, matching corners and sew. This last square forms the crown of your hat.
6. For a prettier finish, do a row of single crochet. It is important that you do 1 sc into every stitch on the edge of the hat plus 1 single crochet in the spaces between the shells. This prevents the edge of the hat from tightening.

Squares sewn in a ring

Notes and Options

This hat may be made for a child by using a G hook and 4 squares around.

130

Granny Square Tote Bag

Rug yarn
    1 large skein antique gold
    1 small skein red
    1 small skein royal blue
    1 small skein olive green
(Cut 3½-yard lengths of each color for
    twisted cord handle)
Size J crochet hook
15-inch x 30-inch piece of cotton print
    for lining
Embroidery needle
Large tapestry needle
Matching thread
Thimble
Pins
Tape measure

1. Make 2 identical squares (follow general Granny Square directions). For each square make 6 rounds of antique gold, 1 round of red, 1 round of royal blue, and 1 round of olive green. Each square should measure about 14 inches.

2. For the outside row, tie on gold yarn between shells in any corner. Work a single crochet stitch in each stitch of row below, completely around. In each corner stitch, work three single crochets. Fasten off yarn.

3. Place and pin right sides of squares together. With tapestry needle and gold yarn, overcast the two squares on three sides. Put this outer bag aside while you make the liner.

4. To make the granny tote bag liner: Fold the fabric in half, printed right sides together, forming a "pocket" 15 inches x 15 inches. To close the side seams, pin ½ inch in from the edges

along the sides next to the folded bag bottom. Sew the side seams with a small Running Stitch or a Backstitch. Insert the liner into the granny tote. (Do not turn the liner inside out.) Fit the bottom of the liner snugly into the bottom of the tote. Fold under a 1-inch hem around the unfinished top of the liner. The hem should face the inside of the granny square. Pin the folded edge around the bag opening just below the last row of single crochet. Join it with an Overcasting Stitch catching the yarn stitches (see overcasting directions page 24).

5. Make a twisted cord of a strand of each of the four colors for a 36-inch length cord to fit over your shoulder. You will need 3½ yards of each color. (See directions for making cord pp. 154.) Take the finished twisted cord and weave it in and out through the spaces in the last row of the Granny Square Tote Bag and tie the two ends together in a knot, leaving a fringe end.

Notes and Options

This tote can also be used as a carry-all or may be attached to the back of a wheelchair.

Granny Square Afghan
(finished size 55 inches x 70 inches)

4-ounce skeins 4-ply worsted or 4-ply Orlon:
  2 skeins color A, for center row 1
  3 skeins color B, for second row
  4 skeins color C, for third row
  7 skeins color D for fourth row and
    border of afghan (main color)
Size J crochet hook
Tapestry needle
Thimble
Pins
Scissors

1. Each unit is made up of 4 rounds and is approximately 5 inches square. This granny afghan consists of 11 (width) x 14 (length) squares, a total of 154 squares.
2. Each square consists of color A center, color B second round, color C third round. Color D, also known as your main color, is the fourth and last round of this square.
3. Pin and overcast (see p. 24) 2 squares with right sides together. Continue in

132

this way until you have sewn 11 squares into a strip. This is the width of your afghan. Make 13 more strips of 11 squares.

4. Now you have to attach one strip to another, carefully matching corners and shells. Repeat the pinning and the overcast. Continue in the same way until all strips are joined.

5. This afghan can be used as is, but it does look better with a border of some kind. The simplest border consists of a row of single crochet done in your main color. Do 1 single crochet into every stitch of the row below *plus* 1 single crochet into the spaces between the shells. In each of the four corners of the afghan (the space be- tween your double shells), make 3 single crochet stitches.

Notes and Options

You can make variations of an afghan:

by changing the number of rounds per square

by changing the sequence of your four selected colors

by making a well-blended mixture of hues (for a multicolored traditional granny appearance)

For all afghans we suggest you buy an additional skein of the main color. This will always be the color of the last round of your squares and your afghan.

10 Knitting

Knitting for the not-so-nimble is the most difficult of the needlecrafts because it requires two-handed dexterity. After studying available needlework books, I cannot emphasize strongly enough, that the not-so-nimble can learn knitting only by observation and practice rather than written instruction. Here, I will give you, however, some of the basics. Your Helping Hand can show you how to hold the needles and yarn, how to "cast on" (place the first row of stitches onto the needle) and how to manipulate the needles for each type of stitch.

The reason for including knitting in this book is that once the basics have been mastered or your Helping Hand has gotten you off to a good start, knitting can become an enjoyable pastime.

Knitting Basics

Needles

A large-eyed, blunt-end tapestry needle is needed for sewing seams together and for weaving in thread ends. For the actual knitting, we recommend medium-sized straight knitting needles. The needle sizes are listed with each project (none smaller than a #4 and none larger than a #13).

Yarns

Four-ply knitting worsted or Orlon or acrylic of the same weight is suggested; rug yarn is used in some projects. Don't forget to buy an ample amount of yarn, and be sure that all dye lot numbers are the same, so that all your yarn of one color won't have the slight variations which sometimes occur from dye lot to dye lot.

Stitch Name	Abbreviation
knit	K
purl	P
increase	inc
decrease	dec
stitch	st

Casting On with One Needle

Measure off approximately 1½ inches of yarn for each stitch to be cast on and make a slip knot at this point on the right-hand needle. Loop the shorter length of yarn around your left thumb, the skein yarn over your index finger and hold the strands in the palm of your left hand. Put the tip of the right needle through the loop on the thumb. Catch the yarn from the skein around the needle from back to front and pull the yarn through the loop. Slip the loop off the thumb and pull the stitch just made onto the right knitting needle. Continue for the required number of stitches.

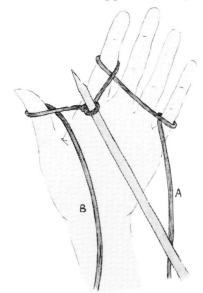

Position of hands for casting on, step 1

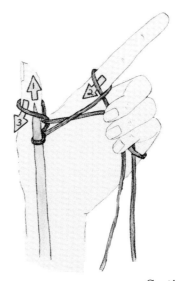

Casting on, step 2

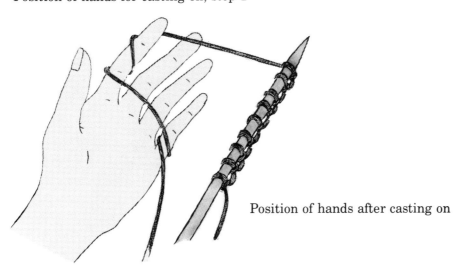

Position of hands after casting on

Knitting

Hold the knitting needle with the cast-on stitches in your left hand. Hold the other needle in your right hand. Keep the yarn from the skein hanging behind the needles. Put the tip of the right hand needle into the first stitch on the left-hand needle (from front to back) and pull the yarn from the skein under and over the top of the right-hand needle, drawing the yarn through the stitch with the needle point. Slip this stitch onto the right-hand needle. Repeat for the required number of stitches.

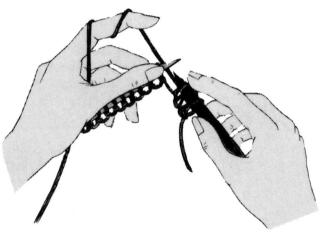

Position of yarn and needles for first knit stitch, step 1

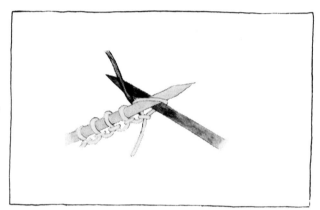

Step 2

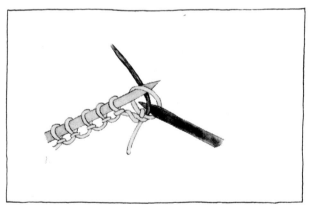

Step 3

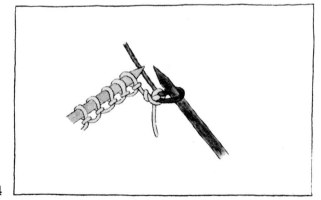

Step 4

Purling

In your left hand hold the needle with the stitches. With the yarn from the skein in front of the needle, put the tip of the right-hand needle into the first stitch (the right needle is in front of the left needle). Catch the yarn from the skein and draw it under the right-hand needle pulling the loop through the stitch on the left-hand needle. Slip the stitch onto the right-hand needle dropping off the loop remaining on the left-hand needle. Repeat for the required number of stitches.

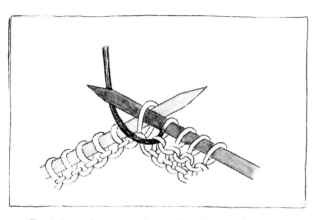

Position of yarn and needles for purl, step 1

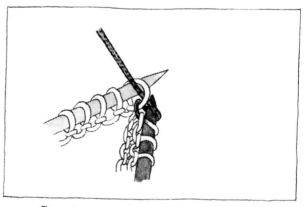

Step 2

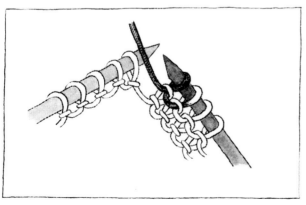

Step 3

Increasing

Knit the first stitch as described in the knitting directions, but do not slip the stitch off the left-hand needle. Knit another stitch into the back of the same stitch on the left needle. You should now have two stitches on your right-hand needle. Pull the left needle out of the second stitch. Repeat for the required number of stitches.

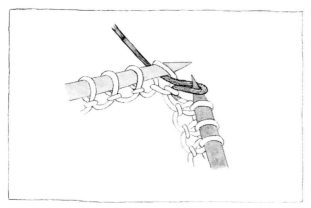

Position of yarn and needles for increasing in the middle of a row, step 1

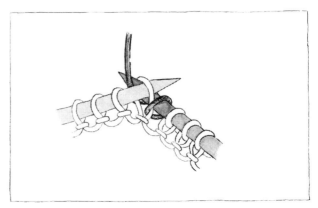

Step 2

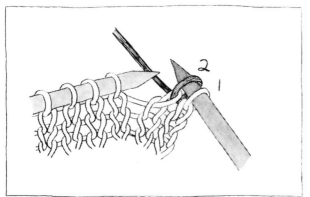

Completed increase at beginning of a knitted section

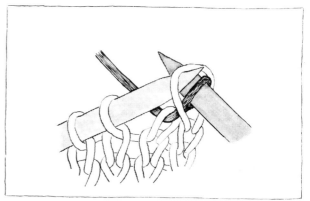

Binding off

Decreasing

Insert your needle into two stitches at the same time and knit them together. Slip the one resulting stitch to your right-hand needle. Repeat for the required number of stitches.

Binding Off

Stitches must be "locked" at the end of a piece to prevent raveling. This is accomplished by loosely knitting the first two stitches at the beginning of the final row. Put your left needle tip into the first stitch and pull it over the second stitch and off the needle. Repeat this until only one stitch remains on the right needle. Cut the yarn from the skein leaving a 6-inch tail hanging. Pull this yarn through the last stitch until it is locked. To bind off in purling, do exactly the same thing except that you purl the stitches instead of knitting them. Weave in any loose ends of yarn.

Colors

There is a tremendous choice of colors and textures. Remember to choose materials that appeal to your eye. Again, don't forget that ombrés, variegated, and tweed yarns can be interesting to work with and camouflage minor errors.

Joining Yarns

It is preferable to attach the yarn at the end of a row. However, you may occasionally run out in the middle of the row. Tie the two ends into an overhand knot, leaving a 2-inch end. When you have completed the project, thread the loose ends into a tapestry needle and weave them neatly into your work on the wrong side.

Sewing Seams

For sewing seams, pin the edges together, matching rows carefully. Thread a tapestry needle with matching yarn and overcast edges with medium tension. (See p. 24.)

None of the items in this section requires blocking.

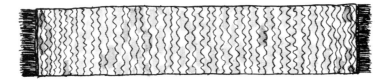

Ombré Scarf
(finished size 8 inches x 48 inches)

2 packs of 3½-ounce skeins knitting worsted ombré
1 pair of #13 knitting needles

1. Cast on 30 stitches.
2. Knit on every row.
3. Continue knitting until the scarf measures 48 inches (you may vary the length).
4. Bind off and weave in the loose ends of yarn.

Notes and Options

Fringe can be added to the ends. (See p. 151.)

Hanger Covers

Cotton or synthetic rug yarn (one 6-ounce skein (145 yards) makes 6 covers)
Wooden hangers
1 pair of #8 knitting needles
#13 tapestry needle (large-eyed, blunt point)
Scissors
Pins
Colored adhesive tape

1. Cast on 10 stitches. This cover should be about 3½ inches wide.
2. Knit each row until you have 42 rows.
3. Bind off.

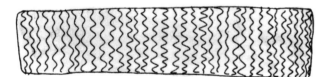

Flat view before inserting hanger

4. Find the center of your knitted piece by folding it in half lengthwise and carefully slipping it over the hanger hook.
5. Pin the bottom edges so they fit around the hanger. Thread a tapestry needle with the same yarn you've used in your knitting and sew the cover together using an Overcast Stitch (see p. 24). Make sure that you sew the ends securely.
6. To finish this project, use colored adhesive tape to wind around the hanger hook.

Notes and Options

These covers are practical for hangers on which you hang knit clothes because they protect them from the sharp corners of ordinary hangers.

To embellish this easy project, add some small artificial flowers, a sachet bag, a ribbon bow, or a bright tassel at the base of the hook.

Triangular Head Scarf
(finished size 23 inches x 23 inches x 33 inches)

Two 3-ounce skeins of mohair acrylic yarn
#10 knitting needles

1. With #10 knitting needles, cast on 130 stitches. (This pattern requires knitting every row; this is called the garter stitch.)
2. In the first row, knit across in every stitch (130 stitches).
3. In row 2, knit across until there are 2 stitches remaining on the left-hand needle. Knit these 2 stitches together (a decrease).
4. Continue repeating step 3 for all rows—decreasing 1 stitch at the end of every row until 3 stitches remain on the needle. Bind these 3 stitches off loosely.

Notes and Options

You can add a crocheted edge or a short fringe on the two shorter sides for a decorative effect.

Watch Cap for Child

One 4-ounce skein of knitting worsted
1 pair #8 knitting needles
Tapestry needle

1. Cast on 80 st.
2. K1, P1, for 4 inches.
3. Change to stockinette st (K 1 row, P 1 row) until whole piece is 8½ inches long.
4. Then K 2 st together across row (40 st left)
   P 1 row
   K 2 st together across row (20 st left)
   P 1 row
   K 2 st together across row (10 st left)
   P 1 row
5. Cut yarn, leaving an 18-inch length. Thread yarn needle and run thread

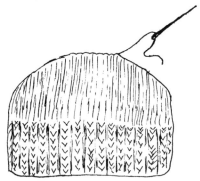

Flat view of yarn before sewing

through all stitches on knitting needle. Pull stitches together tightly and tie yarn well.

View of top pulled and sides ready to be sewn

6. Place the right sides together, pin first and then sew, using a Running Stitch or a Backstitch. Do not make your stitches too tight. Stitch to within 3 inches of end of the piece. Now turn hat inside out and stitch the last 3 inches on the right side. Turn up a 3-inch cuff.

Notes and Options

This cap may be trimmed with a multicolor or solid color fat tassel. (See p. 152.)

Watch Cap for Adult

One 4-ounce skein of knitting worsted
1 pair #8 knitting needles
Tapestry needle

1. Cast on 100 st.
2. K1, P1, for 6 inches.
3. Change to stockinette st (K 1 row, P 1 row) until whole piece measures 9½ inches.
4. Then K 2 st together across row (50 st left)
   P 1 row
   K 2 st together across row (25 st left)
   P 1 row
   K 2 st together across row (13 st left)
   (There will be a single stitch at the end.)
   P 1 row
5. Cut yarn, leaving a 20-inch length. Thread yarn needle and run thread through all remaining 13 stitches on knitting needle. Pull stitches together tightly and tie yarn well.
6. Place the right sides together, pin first and then sew, using a Running Stitch or a Backstitch. Do not make your stitches too tight. Stitch to within 3 inches of end of the piece. Now turn hat inside out and stitch the last 3 inches on the right side. Turn up a 3-inch cuff.

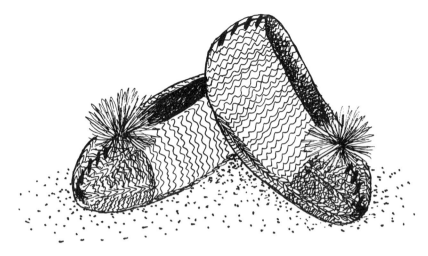

Soft Slippers

One 4-ounce skein knitting worsted
1 pair #8 knitting needles
Tapestry needle

1. Using two strands of knitting worsted held together throughout, cast
   on 32 st.
2. Row 1, K10, P1, K10, P1, K10.
3. Row 2, knit across.
4. Repeat these 2 rows for 21 ridges
   (woman's size); 19 ridges (child); 16

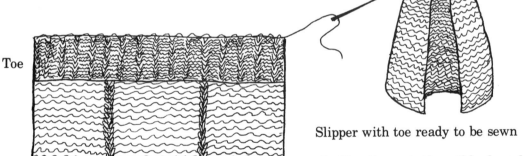

Flat view before sewing

ridges (toddler). A ridge consists of 2
knitted rows.
5. K1, P1 (ribbing) for 3 inches.
6. Cut yarn, leaving a 12-inch length.

Thread a tapestry needle with this
yarn and pull through all stitches on
knitting needle. Tie the stitches together tightly. A tiny hole will be left
at front.

Slipper with toe ready to be sewn

7. Starting at the ribbed end, sew up
   front ribbing to form front seam.
8. Sew back seam evenly.

Notes and Options

These slippers may be worn on carpet
to prevent slipping.

You can adorn the toe of the slipper by
adding a tassel or pompom (see pp. 152
and 153).

144

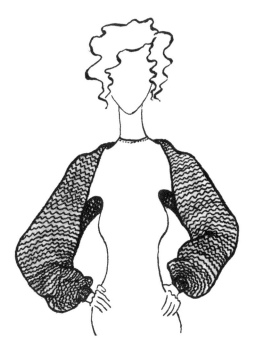

Shoulder Sweater

Two 4-ounce skeins of knitting worsted
1 pair #4 knitting needles
1 pair #10 knitting needles

1. Cast on 40 st on #4 needles.
2. K2, P2, for 3 inches (this will make the ribbed cuff).
3. Increase in every other st across row (60 st).
4. Change to #10 needles and knit (60 st on) each row until desired length.
5. Measure (by trying on) shoulderette before starting second cuff.
6. Change to #4 needles.
7. Decrease 1 st every other st across row (40 st).
8. K2, P2, for 3 inches.
9. Bind off loosely.
10. At each end, matching carefully, overcast a seam measuring 12 inches from cuff through garter stitch (knitted every row) part of shoulderette (see below).

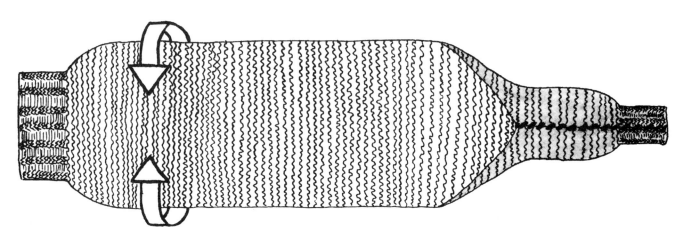

Flat view showing how to sew sleeves

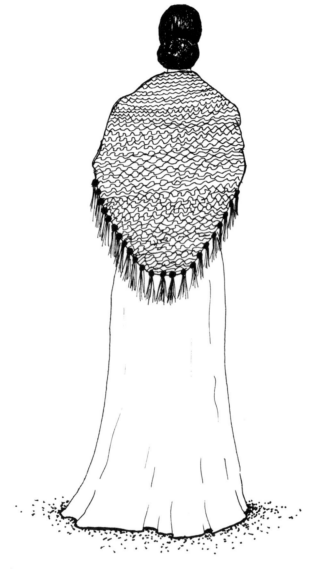

Large Triangular Shawl

Nine 2-ounce skeins of 3-ply acrylic
  mohair or five 4-ounce skeins knitting
  worsted
#13 knitting needles, 14-inch length

Size J crochet hook
Scissors
6-inch x 6-inch piece of cardboard for
  fringe

For casting on, pull out 12 yards of yarn from the skein to determine where to place your slip knot. Let the yarn lie on the table as you work it onto the knitting needle (any excess yarn can be cut off and used for fringe). This pattern calls for knitting every row (this is called the garter stitch).

1. Cast on 175 stitches with #13 needles.
2. Row 1, knit across in every stitch (175 stitches).
3. Row 2, knit across until there are 2 stitches remaining on the left-hand needle. Knit these 2 stitches together (a decrease).
4. Continue repeating step 3 for 125 rows.
5. On the next row, knit 2 stitches together at *each end* of the row.
6. Repeat step 5 until 10 stitches are left on the needle.
7. Bind these 10 stitches off loosely.
8. Add fringe along the two shorter sides of the triangle. We suggest 3 strands thick and 12 inches long (see fringe directions p. 151). Put J crochet hook through each decrease stitch at the ends of each row to attach the fringe to the shawl edge.

Rake loom and hook

Rake Loom Knitting

If you ever made a horse rein as a youngster, you will recall how quickly you got results from slipping the yarn over the metal hoops on the wooden spool. You made miles of multicolored tubular knit strips which you probably sewed together for dolls' rugs. This idea has been developed into the rake loom. This loom is an oval frame (about 12 inches long) with raised pegs around which yarn is wound and worked off with a crochet hook or a curved pick. The result of this "picking off" is a knit strip which can be made into scarves, afghans, and even sweaters and hats. The benefit of working on the rake loom is that it does not require the dexterity necessary for knitting with needles; therefore it may be used as a substitute for knitting by the not-so-nimble.

This loom can be purchased at many variety stores or needlework departments for about two dollars. The package contains clear, concise directions for its use.

In addition to the loom and yarn, you need only a tapestry needle to end your work and a crochet hook if you wish to add fringe to your project.

If you are a beginner, I suggest that you make a scarf. You can use a solid color, variegated yarn or multicolored stripes (a good use for leftover yarn). Four-ply worsted, Orlon, or acrylic of the same weight is suitable. Fringing the ends will add an attractive note.

You will use about 2 yards of yarn for each row.

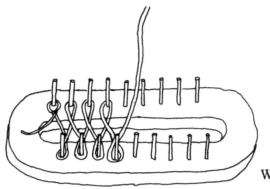

Wrapping the yarn

Rake or Knit-Loom Scarf
(finished size 5 feet long)

1 Bucilla Knit Loom with pick
Two 3-ounce skeins of 4-ply ombré wool
  or synthetic yarn
Size I crochet hook
#18 tapestry needle
6-inch x 6-inch cardboard for fringe
Scissors
Ruler

1. Make a slip loop 3 inches from the yarn end and slip it over the first peg in the upper left corner of the loom. Wind the yarn from the skein around the remaining pegs in a figure-8-type twist following the manufacturer's directions. (Do not wind the yarn too tightly around the pegs.)
2. Turn the loom so that the lower row of pegs becomes the upper row and the yarn from the skein is at the left side.
3. Wind the second row of yarn over the first row.
4. Starting at the right side, work off the loops on the loom by inserting the pick under the lower loop on the first peg in the lower row and slip it over the top loop and off the peg. Repeat across the row.
5. Turn the loom so that the yarn from the skein is on the left end. Leave a single loop on the first peg at right, slip lower loop over the top loop and off each top of each remaining peg to the left end of the loom. One row is now completed. Do not turn the loom. Repeat steps 3 to 5 once for each additional row required. 156 rows will make a 5-foot scarf.

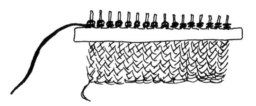

Rake loom scarf in work

6. To bind off, there must be one loop on each peg. Thread the tapestry needle with contrasting color yarn or heavy thread. Beginning at end opposite "working" end of yarn, insert needle in first loop on lower row of pegs, slip loop off peg and on to thread, insert needle in first loop on upper row of pegs and slip on to thread, *slip next loop on lower row, then next loop on upper row to thread; repeat from * until all loops are on thread. Slip yarn from slot and break, leaving 6-inch end. Remove loom. Beginning at end opposite the 6-inch end, insert

a crochet hook into first 2 loops on thread, draw second loop through first loop, † insert hook into next loop and draw it through loop on hook; repeat from † until one loop remains on hook, draw 6-inch end through this loop and fasten off. Remove thread.

If desired, work 1 row slip stitch or single crochet lower edge, working to same tension as strip. Narrower strip may be made by not working across all pegs.

New end of yarn must always be joined at edge of piece. Tie new yarn securely to end of yarn in use.

7. To make fringe, wind yarn around a 6-inch cardboard (see our directions, p. 151). Knot a 4-strand fringe along the cast-on edge, knotting 1 fringe through the 3 loose strands at each "raised" stitch. Knot fringe on the bound-off edge to correspond with the opposite scarf end. Trim the fringes evenly.

11 Trimmings

Fringe

Yarn
Crochet hook
6–8-inch piece of cardboard
Scissors
Ruler

1. Wind a moderate quantity (about 36 inches) of yarn around a piece of cardboard. Do not wind it too tightly.

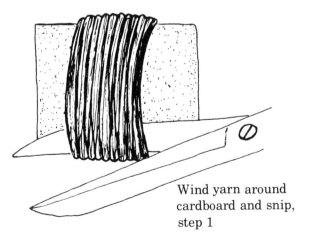

Wind yarn around cardboard and snip, step 1

The width of the cardboard determines the length of the fringe. The length of the cardboard should be about 6 to 8 inches for easy handling.

2. Cut the yarn at one edge only. If you place a book across the end not to be

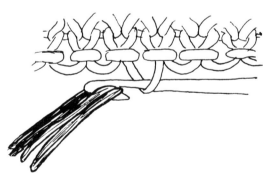

Step 2, crochet hook drawing yarn through edge

cut, it will prevent the yarn from moving. The strands are now twice the final length.

Step 3, crochet hook drawing yarn through edge

3. Take the crochet hook and insert it into the stitch to be fringed. Place the center of 2 cut strands over the hook. Pull the hook and yarn through the stitch for 1 inch. This forms a small loop. Remove the crochet hook.

4. Gather all 4 of the cut strands and

draw them through the eye of the loop you have just created. Pull taut.

5. Repeat this for the length of the piece to which you're adding fringe. We suggest for our projects, that 2 strands of fringe in every other knit or crochet stitch is adequate.

Step 4, tightening the knot

Tassels

1 skein of yarn
6-inch x 6-inch piece of cardboard
Tapestry needle
Scissors
Ruler

1. Wind the yarn 10 times around the cardboard. (This number can vary depending upon the tassel thickness

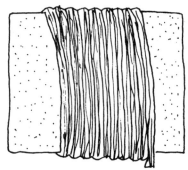

Wind yarn around cardboard

you desire.) Cut off the yarn at the bottom end. (For a 6-inch-long tassel

you need a 3-inch x 6-inch piece of cardboard.)

2. Cut a separate piece of yarn 12 inches long and slip it under the strands on

Tying the yarn at the top

the cardboard. Tie it tightly together at the top (see diagram).

3. Slide the tied, looped strands off the cardboard.

Tightening and slipping the loops off the cardboard

4. Cut another 12-inch piece of yarn.
5. Starting about 1 inch below the top, wrap this tightly around the strands 6 times. Secure it with a double knot and hide the ends in the body of the

Pompom

1-ounce skein of yarn
Tapestry needle
Scissors
12-inch ruler or 1½-inch x 6-inch piece of cardboard

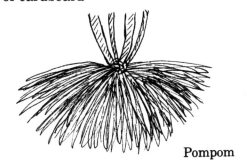

Pompom

Making an authentic pompom requires more dexterity than the not-so-nimble person may have, so we have devised a simplified solution to the problem. This easier method is to make two short, very fat tassels and tie them together at the base to form a pompom.

tassel. Now, snip the bottom (see diagram).
6. Even off all ends and attach it to your work by threading a needle with the 2 strands of yarn you have left over at the top of the tassel.

1. To make each tassel, follow the directions and diagrams for tassel making in the preceding project. The only change is that you wind the yarn around the ruler or cardboard about 50 times.
2. Cut a 12-inch length of yarn and thread the needle with it. Slide the needle and yarn under all the wound yarn on the ruler.
3. Remove the needle from the yarn. Draw the two ends of the yarn under the loops together, as tightly as possible, and tie them into a double knot.
4. Slide the tied yarn off the ruler and cut open the bottom loops.
5. After finishing the two tassels, tie them together at the knotted ends.
6. Trim the fringe ends evenly and attach pompoms where they are needed.

Twisted Cord

4-ply yarn, solid or mixed colors
Scissors
Tape measure

1. The finished product will be twice the thickness of the original number of strands, as the yarn is doubled over. Six strands of 4-ply yarn are adequate for most cord trimmings.
2. Measure the required yardage for the project and multiply that length by 3½ to obtain the length of yarn to cut. For example, if you have a 12-inch pillow to trim, measure around the four sides to get 48 inches x 3½ equals 168 inches, or approximately 5 yards of each strand.

Folding cord in half after twisting

bring the two knotted ends together and hold them. The remainder of the cord will intertwine.

5. Smooth out any irregular twists in the cord by pulling along the length of it with your hand.

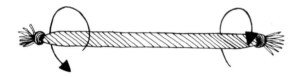

Turning yarn in opposite directions

3. After the strands are cut, line them up neatly and tie a knot at each end.
4. If you have a Helping Hand, she holds one end and you hold the opposite end. Each of you twists your own end of the strands in opposite directions. You may have to stand far apart from one another, as the yarn must be kept taut as you turn it. After the cord is tightly twisted,

Close-up of doubled twisted cord

6. The cord is now ready to be sewn on where needed.

Notes and Options

If you do not have a Helping Hand, hook one knotted end over a doorknob and twist the yarn. Finish off as above.

This cord can also be used as a tote bag handle or as a belt. It is most attractive when it is made up in various colors.

Appendix I

Project Categories

Bed Comfort

Heating Pad Cover . . . . .Sewing
Bedside Holder . . . . .Sewing
Cylinder Bolster Cover . . . . . . .Sewing
Granny Square Afghan . . . . . . .Crochet
Soft Slippers . . . . .Knitting

Carry-Alls

Reversible Kerchief Bag . . . . . . .Sewing
Patchwork Tote Bag . . . . .Quilting
Granny Square Tote Bag . . . . . .Crochet
Bargello Tote Bag . . . . .Needlepoint

Children's Items

Printed Doll . . . . .Sewing
Pocket Wall Hanging . . . . .Sewing
Reversible Kerchief Bag . . . . . . .Sewing
Bouncing Frog or Butterfly . . . .Sewing
Blossoms in a Bowl Wall
    Hanging . . . . .Appliqué

Round Felt Flower Pillow . . . .Appliqué
Quick Trim Embroidery . . .Embroidery
Apple Patch . . . . .Appliqué
Baby Coverlet . . . . . . .Simple Weaving
Baby Quilt . . . . .Quilting
Child's Granny Square Hat . . . .Crochet
Child's Red Crochet Hat . . . . . . .Crochet
Watch Cap for a Child . . . . . .Knitting
Soft Slippers . . . . .Knitting
Triangular Head Scarf . . . . . . .Knitting

Home Decorations

Set of Four Place Mats . . . . .Sewing
Cactus Pincushion . . . . .Sewing
Mirror Mat on Counted-Thread
    Fabric . . . . .Embroidery
Place Mats on Counted-Thread
    Fabric . . . . .Embroidery
Cross Stitch on Gingham Place
    Mats . . . . .Embroidery

Double Cross Stitch Jute
    Rug . . . . .Embroidery
Small Bargello Rug . . . . . . .Needlepoint
Picture Frame . . . . .Needlepoint

Pillows, Pictures, and Wall Hangings

These items may be finished as pillows, framed as pictures or hung as banners.

Cylinder Bolster Cover . . . . .Sewing
Washcloth Pillow . . . . .Sewing
"Picasso" Owl in Felt . . . . . .Embroidery
Starflower Pillow . . . . .Embroidery
Sun in a Hoop . . . . .Embroidery
Blossoms in a Bowl Wall
    Hanging . . . . .Appliqué
Frankly Fake Felt Flower
    Picture . . . . .Appliqué
Nosegay Picture . . . . .Appliqué
Round Felt Flower Pillow . . . .Appliqué
Lion's Head Pillow . . . . .Quilting
Contemporary Patch
    Picture . . . . .Needlepoint
Half Cross Stitch
    Geometric Pillow . . . . . . .Needlepoint
Rainbow-Striped Pillow . . .Needlepoint
Raised Cross Stitch Rose
    Pillow . . . . .Novelty Stitches
Shaggy Sunflower
    Pillow . . . . .Novelty Stitches
Splash of Color Rya
    Pillow . . . . .Novelty Stitches

Quick and Easy to Give or Keep

Cactus Pincushion . . . . .Sewing
Heating Pad Cover . . . . .Sewing
Washcloth Pillow . . . . .Sewing
"Picasso" Owl on Felt . . . . .Embroidery
Quick Trim Embroidery . . .Embroidery
Apple Patch . . . . .Appliqué
Embroidered Belt on Rug
    Canvas . . . . .Needlepoint
Plastic Mesh Key Ring
    Tag . . . . .Needlepoint
Picture Frame . . . . .Needlepoint
Hanger Covers . . . . .Knitting

Wearables

Cape Shawl . . . . .Sewing
Weave-Through
    Shawl . . . . .Simple Weaving
Embroidered Belt on Rug
    Canvas . . . . .Needlepoint
Long Scarf . . . . .Crochet
Sleeveless Vest . . . . .Crochet
Granny Square Hat . . . . .Crochet
Ombré Scarf . . . . .Knitting
Triangular Head Scarf . . . . . .Knitting
Watch Cap for Child . . . . .Knitting
Watch Cap for Adult . . . . .Knitting
Soft Slippers . . . . .Knitting
Shoulder Sweater . . . . .Knitting
Large Triangular Shawl . . . . .Knitting
Rake or Knit-Loom Scarf . . . .Knitting

Appendix II

Shopping Information

Many of these products may be found in craft shops, needlework shops, variety stores, and through mail order catalogues. Two catalogues we recommend are obtainable from:

1. Merribee Needlecraft Company
   1297 Massachusetts Avenue
   Arlington, Massachusetts 02174
2. Lee Ward
   1200 St. Charles Street
   Elgin, Illinois 60120

I. Self-Help Aids

A. Needle threaders
   1. Wire needle threader with magnifying glass:
      Scovill-Dritz Manufacturing Company
      Spartanburg, South Carolina 20301
   2. Needle threader with handle:
      Merribee Needlecraft Company
      1297 Massachusetts Avenue
      Arlington, Massachusetts 02174
   3. Automatic needle threader:
      Reston Manufacturing Company
      Naugatuck, Connecticut 06770
B. Yarn threader:
   1. Muriel's Needlecraft Company, Inc.
      P. O. Box 12
      Fitchburg, Massachusetts 01420
C. Magnifier (neck strap):
   1. Hoffritz
      20 Cooper Square
      New York, New York 10003

II. Supplies

A. Bag handles
   1. Merribee Needlecraft Company
      1297 Massachusetts Avenue
      Arlington, Massachusetts 02174

157

2. Lee Ward
   1200 St. Charles Street
   Elgin, Illinois 60120
B. Wooden bag handles:
   1. John Dritz and Sons
      350 Fifth Avenue
      New York, New York 10001
C. Bucilla Knit (Rake) Loom:
   Can be found in many needlework
   departments or variety stores.
D. Iron-on bonding material or fusible
   webbing:
   1. Stitch Witchery
      Stacy Fabrics
      469 7th Avenue
      New York, New York 10018
   2. Poly Web (Coats and Clark)
      Woolworths
E. Fasteners
   Flexible Nylon Fabric Fasteners:
   Trade names: Velcro and Scotchmate
   Fabric Fasteners
   Available in most needlework and
   variety stores.
F. Easy-to-work materials:
   1. Plastic mesh
      Columbia-Minerva Corporation
      295 5th Avenue
      New York, New York 10016

2. Counted-thread fabrics:
   Art Needlework Treasure Trove
   P. O. Box 2440
   Grand Central Station
   New York, New York 10017

   Needlecraft Shop
   4501 Van Nuys Boulevard
   Sherman Oaks, California 91403

   Selma's Art Needlework
   1645 Second Avenue
   New York, New York 10028

   Ball of Yarn
   1208 Gordon Street
   Charlotte, North Carolina 28205
G. Hot-iron transfer pencil:
   Merribee Needlework Company
   1297 Massachusetts Avenue
   Arlington, Massachusetts 02174
H. Printed dolls and animals:
   Local fabric shops
   For old-fashioned cat, dog, and doll
     write to:
   Museum of the City of New York
   Fifth Avenue and 104th Street
   New York, New York 10029

INDEX